Sue Plumtree is the joint owne.
'Entre Nous', a company form ... to help people to
forge and develop more fulfilling relationships. An
experienced personnel specialist and a Fellow of the
Institute of Personnel and Development, she heads
her own management training business, developing
and conducting communication and interpersonal
skills courses for national and international companies in the UK, Europe and the USA. Her extremely
successful workshops entitled *'What to do when
someone takes your fancy'* form the basis for much of
the information in this book.

Of Viennese extraction, Sue was raised in Buenos
Aires, has been married to an Englishman for
twenty-nine years, and lives in Hertfordshire.

A special thank you to Simone Klass my friend and joint partner in *Entre Nous*, whose idea it was to write this book and without whom it would not have been written.

ACROSS A CROWDED ROOM

How to find and keep the love of your life

SUE PLUMTREE

Headline

First published in 1995
by HEADLINE BOOK PUBLISHING

10 9 8 7 6 5 4 3 2 1

ISBN 0 7472 4789 7

Typeset by
Letterpart Limited, Reigate, Surrey

Printed and bound in Great Britain by
Cox & Wyman Ltd, Reading, Berks

HEADLINE BOOK PUBLISHING
A division of Hodder Headline PLC
338 Euston Road
London NW1 3BH

Meine geliebteste Prinzessin, Du bist meine
allerbeste Freundin und ich widme dieses Buch an
Dich und an unserem geliebten Papuscam.

My dearest Princess, you are my very best friend
and I dedicate this book to you and our dear Dad.

CONTENTS

Introduction

Introduction

What is our deepest desire? What do we want more than anything else in the world, irrespective of our sex, age, nationality, colour, state of health or how rich or poor we are? The answer is we want to love and to be loved, we want to feel close to someone special, to feel known, accepted and cared for.

Is it because being in love is so exciting? Because there's no doubt about it: being in love is one of life's greatest thrills! Have you noticed how people always seem to be able to tell when we're in love? There's a spring in our step, we smile more, we're nicer to others. If you're a woman, your friends will comment that you look positively radiant! This is a terrific beginning, but as you no doubt know, the fever cools. If we're lucky – and in this book I will show you how to become lucky – what remains is a deep, fulfilling and enduring love, the kind of love that enables us to show that person that they truly matter to us and, hopefully, we will know that we truly matter to them too.

This is the kind of loving that gives meaning to our lives, it keeps us warm when it's cold outside, it makes us feel valued, special and strong. With this kind of love to sustain us, we can handle anything life throws at us.

If you're already misty-eyed with excitement and raring to go, hold on a moment because there's more. Unless you're very young, you will already have some unhappy relationships behind you. Were you just unlucky? Did you choose the wrong person? Are you still humming the song *Some day my prince – or princess – will come*, hoping that next time you will strike lucky? Well, let me tell you, luck plays only a small part; you play a much bigger one, because there's so much that you can do.

I know what you're thinking, 'Well, if I've got all that ability to make things happen, how come nothing's happening? Why do I feel so lonely, so isolated? Why do I feel that my social life is in a rut, why can't I go out and make friends? How come everybody is paired off except me?' If that's what you feel then, believe me, you're not alone. In fact, this is more common than you might think. Since I started running my workshop 'What to Do When Someone Takes Your Fancy', I have found that the men and women who attend are generally attractive, interesting and successful at work. If you saw them you would think that they've got nothing to worry about and wonder why they bothered to come along at all. In the beginning I used to wonder too. Now I know better.

The reasons why people feel uninspired by their social life vary. Some have been too busy with work, others feel more comfortable dealing with people in a business context where their job title, status, and the name of their company give them the confidence they lack in social situations. Others may be newly single and not sure how or where to start. And then there are those who are a little shy and unsure of themselves. The one thing most of them have in common is fear of rejection. Does this ring any bells for you? If it does, then let me give you some encouraging information.

Over the last couple of decades, social scientists have been carrying out vast amounts of research into what attracts people to one another, how to develop intimacy, what makes or breaks relationships – both love and friendships – what's so special about couples who have been happily together for many years, and so on.

The reason I set up my workshop to help people navigate these tricky waters is because fulfilling relationships play an enormously important role in our lives. Psychologists have come to the conclusion that those of us who have a fulfilling and loving relationship as well as a number of close and supportive friends, are happier, healthier, are better able to handle life's ups and downs, and even live longer.

In this book which is based on my workshop, I will take you through the maze of starting, growing and keeping relationships. I will also talk about what happens to established relationships, what makes them work, what threatens them and, more importantly, what you can do about it. The reason I've done so is because there's a lot of evidence that suggests that the seeds of divorce are sown at the very beginning, when the couple first meet. This sounds plausible to me for a very good reason. We all know that sometimes we enter relationships we suspect are really not good for us, but we either hope that things will change (they never do) or else we're afraid of being alone.

Research has found that, where a marriage runs aground, reasons usually include issues such as jealousy and lack of trust – founded or unfounded; money – lack of it or differences in the way each partner wants to spend it; differences in the way the couple like to spend their free time; disagreements about friends and family – his or hers; being put down in front of friends; nagging and being critical; being taken for granted; or perhaps even mental, emotional or physical abuse. The interesting thing is that all the clues were there at the dating stage! But, while the signs are there, you must be willing to see them. Please note I said *willing* and not *able*. For me, the distressing part is that, even though the signs and the doubts are there, so many of you still go ahead and tie the knot hoping that, magically, things will somehow be 'all right on the night'. They won't. Please, please, believe me. *They won't.*

Why then do we do things that are obviously harmful to our happiness and well-being? Obviously, we don't do it deliberately. What happens is that we enter relationships with a lot of 'baggage', beliefs about ourselves, other people and the world, that affect the way we treat not only others but ourselves as well. Some examples of beliefs that can either enhance the quality of our lives or sabotage it are: 'People are out to screw you'; 'People are mostly good'; 'Other people have all the luck'; 'I have terrific friends'; 'I always end up with losers'; 'Life is full of opportunities'; 'Nothing exciting ever happens to me'; 'Every day is filled with little pleasures, all you have to do is see them'; 'Life is tough'; 'Life is what you make it' and so on. Then there are other kinds of beliefs that affect how we see ourselves or members of the opposite sex. Beliefs such as 'I'm too fat and nobody likes fat people', 'I'm an attractive person', 'I'm boring', 'People enjoy my company', 'I need a man to look after me and make me happy', 'I'm a loyal friend,' 'A woman is nothing without a man', 'Although I'd prefer to be in a relationship I don't desperately need one', 'All women are just after a fat wallet', 'Men are just as vulnerable as women. We all try to do the best we can even if we sometimes screw up' (and vice versa!), and so on.

The trouble is that, more often than not, we're not even aware that we hold these beliefs and that's why, if we hold negative beliefs, we always seem to land ourselves in the same unhappy situations, why we seem to attract the same kinds of people who are no good for us. On the other hand, if we hold positive beliefs, we stand a much better chance of developing fulfilling relationships because we are more tolerant of ourselves and others.

Once you start to experiment with new ways of doing things, you will need to be aware of some of the barriers that may get in your way, and I will be discussing them in Chapters 8 and 10 – Expectations: They Can Make Your Relationship Fail! and What Attracts People to One Another? Other things that will help you along the way are your willingness to invest some time to clarify your needs, preferences and values, and to get to know people well, especially your potential partner. (See Chapters 17 and 18 – How to Recognise the Right Partner for You and What Do You Say After You Say 'Hello'?.)

Many of our disappointments are unnecessary. That's why I'm such a firm believer in the principle 'start as you mean to go on', and many of the ideas in this book will help you do just that. But don't attempt everything at once. It's too much to handle in one go. Just try one or two things at a time, see how they work, change them to suit your style, and carry on practising them until you feel comfortable. Then try something else. Once you start getting results, you'll see a whole new world opening up before you!

Of course, people are unpredictable, and I can't guarantee that every single idea will work with every single person all the time. But what I can give you is a toolkit of insights, ideas and skills that will help you to experiment with new and more productive ways of doing things so that, if you try something which doesn't quite work, you will have other avenues to explore.

We all have the power to learn and to take control of our life. I know that starting to make changes can make us feel anxious and vulnerable, but the ideas in this book really work. They will help you get things off the ground in such a way that you can increase the odds of developing fulfilling friendships and love relationships. Once you get started – actually *doing* rather than wishing – you will find that things begin to gather momentum. When we tackle things that make us feel a little scared, and find we've survived the attempt, we get a tremendous sense of achievement that makes us feel great about ourselves – and that, in turn, begins to affect other areas of our life.

Changing the habits of a lifetime takes time and determination. So, please don't get discouraged and don't give up! It's only when you persevere that you will see a difference – maybe not tomorrow or the day after, but if you persist, results will come. I guarantee it!

I have a question that I want you to ask yourself:

DO YOU WANT TO CONTINUE TO ACCEPT WHATEVER IS DISHED
OUT TO YOU, OR DO YOU WANT TO DECIDE WHAT YOU WANT
AND THEN GO FOR IT?

If you prefer the second alternative, start using the ideas, tips and insights from this book now – today! Don't delay! You are embarking on a voyage of discovery. *Bon voyage* – and have fun!

CHAPTER 1

What Do People Want?

When we meet people who have a wide circle of friends, we like to assume that they are either lucky or that they have just been born with that special 'something' that attracts people. Much research has gone into trying to identify the magic ingredient that makes one person attractive to lots of people while another one just sits and watches from the sidelines. But there is no magic ingredient – and research is beginning to identify the various factors that contribute to success with people. In particular, they have pinpointed four elements:

1. Self-esteem
2. Taking the initiative
3. Being aware of what people do that attracts them to one another
4. Being socially skilled

This book is about these four factors – and more.

People come to my workshops because they are looking for help in a number of specific areas that fall under four main headings:

A. They want to learn specific skills, such as:
- How to approach someone they don't know
- How to start and sustain a meaningful conversation
- How to develop closeness
- How to project a 'warmer' personality

7

B. They want to develop self confidence, and learn:
- How to feel more confident when approaching people
- How to feel more confident when asking someone out
- How to overcome their fear of rejection
- How to handle rejection without losing confidence
- How to improve their self-esteem

C. They want to find out:
- How to make friends with people
- How to recognise when a person of the opposite sex is interested in them
- How and when to go about developing a sexual relationship
- Why people often become paralysed when they see someone who takes their fancy and what to do about it.

D. They want answers to 'burning' questions, such as:
- Why do men say 'I'll call you' and then don't?
- How to work out who pays
- What men and women look for in each other
- How men feel about being asked out.

Getting started

After a while, most of us tend to communicate with our partner, family (and sometimes our friends) in a fairly casual and superficial way, filling in the gaps with assumptions that may long be out of date. This is one of the things that makes them complain that we take them for granted. We tend to assume that we know what they're thinking and feeling and what their views and opinions are, and all without having to check them out. We even assume that they are the same as ours! Then, one day, we wake up and discover that we're living with a stranger. What a waste!

When things go smoothly and our partner or family behave as we expect them to, we regard them as predictable with nothing new to surprise us or shake us out of our complacency. That's when the rot sets in and we start to take them for granted. Meanwhile, over a period of time, we stop seeing their positive points and start homing in on their flaws and, should they displease us in some way, we are quick to criticise. We just seem to notice the things they say and do that don't conform to our expectations, or the things that we regard as negative and unacceptable. This is particularly so with our partner. Clearly then, we need to do two things: review our expectations, and reassess the way we treat and communicate with the people who, supposedly, are important to us.

Perhaps right now you're thinking 'Why is she always picking on me?' or 'I've been telling him for months that he's taking me for granted!' So why do I talk about what we do to others, rather than what they do to us, or even what we do to each other? You may not like to hear this, but the truth is that we cannot change other people without their cooperation and agreement. The only thing we can do is review our own expectations, change the way we treat others and take responsibility for the consequences. That's all there is to it! Simple, isn't it?

But don't despair! In Chapter 24 we will look at self-esteem. Self-image is how we *see* ourselves while self-esteem has to do with how much we *like* ourselves. Both are very important because, if we feel comfortable with who we are, then we are less likely to expect other people to make us happy, because we know how to make ourselves happy. I bet you are surprised at this, because the romantic myth talks about two halves coming together to make a whole. Well, I have news for you. That's all it is, a myth. Only two basically happy and secure people have a good chance of forming a happy relationship. That's because, if we don't really like ourselves, we will always feel insecure and needy, constantly looking for reassurance of the 'Do you love me?' variety. 'Yes, yes, I love you.' 'Yes, but do you really, *really* love me?'

(Exasperated sigh.) 'I knew it! You're going off me!' Who can live with that? Being happy is not a matter of luck either; it's something we can all learn. And there's help with this in Chapter 25, The Art of Being Happy.

Another very important area I will be touching on shortly is that of awareness. Over a period of time, we seem to stop really 'seeing' and 'hearing' the people who presumably are important to us. They're just there, part of the furniture, and so we start taking them for granted. I don't think you will disagree with me when I say that this is a sure-fire recipe for disaster. Let me show you how to reawaken your awareness.

Try the following exercise:

Exercise

1. Start by closing your eyes and imagine that you are in a room with, say, ten people you know (both men and women), such as a couple of family members, one close and one casual friend, a past partner, your boss, one or two colleagues, a subordinate, if you have any, and perhaps one or two people you have met only a couple of times. There's nothing to stop you including the milkman if you feel like it.

2. Now try to conjure them up in your mind's eye, one person at a time, imagining that they're there in the room with you. What I'd like you to do next is to try to 'see' between three and five qualities that you particularly like about each person. (When we first meet people, we're likely to be attracted by things that are different from the ones that will appeal to us once we get to know them better.)

3. As you do this exercise, write down all your ideas. This is very important because writing things down reinforces them while, if you just try to rely on your memory, you will find that after a while they seem to fade away again, and you don't want to be back to where you began.

Here are a few ideas to get you started:

When I first met Sheila, I noticed she had a friendly smile, she always seemed cheerful and had a pleasant word to say to everybody.

In the case of Mark, I have only spoken with him once so far, but what first drew me to him was his friendly smile. Then, once we got talking, I noticed how enthusiastic he was about his work and that he gave credit for some good ideas to other people on his team.

On the other hand, I have known Andrea for some time, and two of the things I really love about her are her infectious giggle and her terrific sense of humour. At the same time, I cherish the fact that she is a very caring listener who doesn't judge or impose her opinions. I can talk to her about anything under the sun, and she sends me funny cards to cheer me up when I'm feeling low.

Then there is my friend John. What I really treasure about him is that he takes the time to truly listen to me, which makes me feel really understood and very special to boot. Also, he tells me the truth, and not what he thinks I want to hear, which he then tempers with practical help, real encouragement and support. And, on top of all that, he cheers me along, celebrating my successes and comforting me when I experience setbacks.

Try to focus on personal qualities. Alternatively, it may help you to think about specific times when you felt really positive towards each of the people on your list and then work out what they were doing or saying that made you feel like that. Don't rush – it really is worth taking your time. You don't have to finish the exercise all in one go, but be sure you go back to it and repeat the process for every person on your list.

This exercise will do three things for you. First, it will make these people 'visible' to you again. Then, it will 'remind' you of your affection for at least those close to you. And finally, it will give you material for the next step, which is described in Chapter 20, In Praise of Praise.

The point of this exercise was nicely made by an analogy I came across recently. Imagine going to a concert. There you may tune into the coughing of the audience. If you do, the sound of the music will fade away. On the other hand, if you concentrate on the music, you may occasionally hear some faint coughing but it won't distract you from the music and the pleasure you get from it.

The principle behind this is absolutely sound and based on solid scientific research: not only do you find what you look for – it also concentrates your thoughts. And thinking positive thoughts about your partner and other people in your life, will help you value them more. From that it follows that you will treat them better, which will make them treat you well in return. It's an unending positive cycle that helps you deal constructively with the ups and downs of every relationship.

Obviously, just because we look out for people's good qualities, that doesn't mean they are flawless or that they won't sometimes do things that hurt, annoy or anger us, and it certainly doesn't mean that we should put up with unacceptable or thoughtless behaviour. Chapter 20 also gives you tips on how to deal with this.

Jean came to one of my workshops shortly after splitting up with Nick, with whom she had been going out for nearly six months. 'At first everything was wonderful,' she told us, 'but then I began to notice things about him that made me feel more and more irritated and critical. We started rowing about little things and the rows became more and more frequent until we finally decided we just weren't suited to each other.' Then she told us that this had happened once or twice before. 'Everything is wonderful at first,' she said, 'and then things go steadily downhill.' She had now met a new man but was afraid it would go the same way as with her previous relationships. While she was doing this exercise, she suddenly remembered something Nick had shouted at her during one of their rows: 'You are always picking on me, looking for faults! Nothing I do is ever right!' That was when she suddenly realised that she had come to take for granted the good things about Nick that had originally drawn her to him – and stopped noticing them. Instead, she had started to become mostly aware of the things that irritated her and that did not meet her expectations. Now that she realised it, she was well on her way to making some important changes.

Keep the principles of this exercise in mind and try to focus on at least two or three things you like about everyone with whom you come into contact. You might need to do a mental somersault because we generally expect people to prove themselves to us before we decide whether or not we're going to like them, but it's certainly worth the effort. Make a conscious decision that you *will* find something to like in everyone you meet; not just in the people you already know, but also in those you have only just met.

Say you have decided to join your local bowling club. You don't know anyone yet. You can either go with the attitude of 'Let's see what kind of people go there', or you can simply decide that you will meet one or two interesting people and that you will have a great time. The operative word here is *will*. That's the kind of approach that attracts people because it makes them feel that they don't have to be especially clever or witty to be accepted – they can just be themselves.

TIPS
- Don't wait for others to change. Start making changes of your own in the way you act, talk and treat people, and they will change in the way they respond to you.

- Focus on two or three qualities that you regard as attractive, appealing or interesting about everyone you know, both in your social life and at work – whether you have only just met them or known them for some time. If you already know them well this exercise will remind you of what made you like or love them in the first place. If you have only just met, it will put you in a positive frame of mind towards them.
- Do this exercise on a regular basis to keep yourself aware of their positive points. It will help you avoid the danger of taking them for granted. The results of doing this could be dramatic!

14

CHAPTER 2

Rejection: A Fate Worse Than Death?

Researchers have discovered that the key factor that stops people from taking the initiative in social contact is fear of rejection. This is the number one fear. However, they also found that rejection was *not* a factor in whether or not a person was socially successful. Let me give you two examples.

Frank works in a bank and has been there for three years. He mentioned that he very rarely shares his lunch break with any of his colleagues and, when I asked him why not, he said that they didn't want to. He told me that he had suggested it once or twice but that all he got was excuses. He took them very much to heart and decided not to ask again. If they wanted to, they could always ask him. He never even considered the possibility that there might have been some good reasons why they couldn't join him on those particular days. He just assumed they weren't interested in him. So he stopped asking.

You couldn't find anyone more different from Frank than Jay. A single parent in her forties, she attracts people like bees to honey. She once told me that one day she would like to meet someone special, but that meanwhile she doesn't go around with a magnifying glass trying to find him. Jay has had more than her fair share of setbacks and works hard to bring up her son single-handedly. However, her positive and optimistic outlook attracts love and affection in the form of friendships of various degrees of closeness with men and women of all ages. When I asked her what her secret was, how come everybody was attracted to her, her reply, after she recovered from a fit of laughter, was that she was most definitely not everybody's cup of tea. 'Honey,' she said, 'there are lots of people who find me too much of a handful but there's plenty of fish in the sea.' Her motto is 'SW – SW – SW – Next!' which translated means 'Some Will, Some Won't, So What! – Next!'

These two examples reflect the results of a study in which researchers interviewed people about whether they saw themselves as socially successful or unsuccessful. What they found was that those who regarded themselves as social successes tended to have a *higher* rate of rejection than those who saw themselves as unsuccessful. The reason for this apparent contradiction was that those who were socially successful, like Jay, took more initiatives and met more people than those who saw themselves as failures, like Frank, but in doing so found that, as Jay put it, they were 'certainly not everybody's cup of tea'.

According to this study, the socially successful recovered more quickly from their setbacks, while the socially unsuccessful tended to give up quicker and after fewer rejections, took setbacks very much to heart and took longer to recover.

There's no doubt that rejections can be hurtful. Let's put this into perspective, though. Everybody, however beautiful, rich or famous has, at one time or another, been rejected and there is no reason on earth why you should be the exception. So, what do you do when you walk up to someone and they simply don't want to know? I'm afraid the only answer I can give you is to accept it, walk away and find someone else who will enjoy chatting with you. What you do *not* do is try to figure out where you went wrong, what he or she could have found obnoxious about you, or why they didn't want to talk with you. That's what our Frank tends to do. He always analyses every interaction to death and usually takes the blame for everything he imagines he did wrong. No wonder he is a little bundle of anxieties and insecurities!

There could be any number of reasons why someone doesn't

respond to you. Let's face it, they might simply not be interested and that's OK, because there are and always will be lots of other people who will be interested in you. Besides, if you're really honest with yourself, you aren't always interested in every single person that comes near you, are you? The real point to bear in mind is that they are not rejecting *you*, because after all they don't even know you. And remember that every time you feel hurt when someone rejects you, you give a stranger the power to dictate how you feel about yourself. Eleanor Roosevelt is credited with saying, 'No one can make you feel inferior without your consent', and this sentiment is just as valid today as it was then.

Please read this sentence again, because it's so important:

NO ONE CAN MAKE YOU FEEL INFERIOR
WITHOUT YOUR CONSENT.

So, what are we all so frightened of? Research has shown that most of us are afraid of not 'coming up to scratch', of being seen as inadequate in some way. I come up against this one again and again in my workshops. Someone once remarked that he was afraid of 'being found out'. Imagine how hard it must have been to admit this in a roomful of strangers. And yet, not only did everyone identify with the feeling, but they felt visibly relieved when they realised that they weren't alone. This admission also brought the group closer together because – and not everyone knows this – people often feel inadequate when they are with someone who appears to be totally confident and in control. That's because they tend to believe that such people couldn't possibly understand what it's like to feel vulnerable. Obviously then, you're not the only one who fears rejection. Hard as it may be for you to even imagine it, chances are that others are just as nervous of you because you seem so 'together'.

What makes us feel so bad is not the rejection itself but our interpretation of it. If you see it as proof that you are not terribly popular, then every new rejection – real or imagined, like Frank's – is likely to strengthen that feeling. In fact, you might even come to the conclusion that the rejection just confirms what you knew all along, namely that you are no good, inadequate, unattractive, undesirable, unlovable and worthless. By the time you finish beating yourself up, you will be ready to join the Foreign Legion, or retire into a convent!

If, on the other hand, you see yourself as someone who is generally attractive, then your reaction to the rejection is likely to be, 'Well, it's just one of those things', no more and no less, and you will merely shrug and move on because there are plenty of people out there looking for someone just like you to make friends with.

Many people have said to me that they can happily talk to anyone, except when they see someone who really takes their fancy. Then their legs turn to jelly and their brains switch off. Joanne was one of them. She came to me deeply frustrated. She had been to a party, she told me, and was immediately attracted to this gorgeous man. 'I then made it a point to talk to everyone in the room to make it look like I was having a really good time. I guess I hoped he would think I was a fun person to know and would want to meet me, but he didn't,' she finished, looking disappointed. When I asked her why she hadn't approached him, she looked horrified. 'I couldn't do that!' she exclaimed. But when I pressed her, the best she could come up with was that she wouldn't have known what to say. (For help with this problem, read Chapter 15 – Do You Come Here Often? and Other Openings to Avoid.

This is a very common complaint and it's worth mentioning especially because, surely, that's exactly what you've been hoping for: to meet someone who does take your fancy! The problem is that, if everyone feels scared and waits for the other person to make the first move, chances are that nothing will happen and everyone will lose out. So what can you do to overcome this fear?

There's only one way to deal with fear of any kind, be it fear of rejection, fear of flying, fear of spiders, fear of open spaces, whatever. You have to confront that fear. Being afraid is OK; what is not OK is to let the fear overwhelm and paralyse you, stopping you from getting what you want in life. The fear will never go away and avoiding facing up to it simply makes it worse. So, the longer you resist, the worse it gets! You confront the fear by slowly and gradually doing the very thing you're afraid of. This is how phobias are treated and it is called 'desensitising'.

So let's take a good look at rejection. Let's face it. Yes, you will be rejected, not once, not twice, but probably a fair number of times, and like everybody else although you won't necessarily like it, I have no doubt whatsoever that you will be able to cope. You have to believe in yourself and in your ability to deal with the occasional disappointment. After all, you're not that fragile. You will get over it. It's really important that you should know that and trust yourself to handle it. At first you may need to work at it but that's true every time you learn to do something in a different way, whatever it may be.

Start with easy situations. For example, in the case of fear of flying, desensitising programmes start with talks about air safety statistics, then by simulated flights until you graduate to the real thing. In the case of approaching people, you might start by chatting with someone of the same sex at your local supermarket queue where you can pay for your shopping and leave, so there's very little risk. The next step up might be starting a chat, still with someone of the same sex, at a party or some other public event, and so on, until eventually you graduate by approaching that gorgeous stranger that you fancy like mad.

In the process of getting rid of your fear you also develop confidence because you discover that you're able to do something you used to be scared of, and crossing that barrier does wonders for your self-esteem. I guarantee it! Your best defence against fear of rejection is to develop a strategy. Without it you will continue to be at the mercy of your demons. To get somewhere – anywhere – you need to have a clear purpose and a plan of action. The magic secret to overcoming fear – any fear, not just fear of rejection – is a well thought out strategy and plan of action.

A good starting point is to think of as many different ways of meeting new people as you can (for more on this, read Chapter 4, Where Are All the Good Men and Women?). Then work out your action plan. For example: smile at the cashier next time you go to the supermarket and exchange a few pleasantries; after doing that several times, you might like to ask them out for coffee. Or: ask Frances of Accounts if she would like to go to the park and share your sandwiches with you (nice idea if it's warm and sunny). With both these examples the real issue is not whether you fancy that person – though you need to find them appealing in some way, even if they're the same sex, otherwise you're unlikely to want to approach them in the first place – but just being friendly.

As part of your strategy, get information about dating agencies, or ask your brother or sister if they know anyone they think you might enjoy meeting. You could even enlist a friend and do this as a project together – that way you could support and encourage each other.

Here's another tip: each time you approach somebody new, give yourself a tangible reward, something personal and enjoyable. You deserve it for having taken one step you used to be afraid of – that's certainly worth celebrating. It needn't be time-consuming, big or expensive. What is a good reward? Anything that makes you feel good! The idea is to give yourself a pat on the back, a 'Well done!' from yourself to yourself.

TIPS

- It's OK to be afraid. It's not OK to let fear stop you from getting what you want.
- Accept that you will have your fair share of disappointments, setbacks and rejections, but remember: *You can handle them!*
- Beneath a confident exterior most people feel just as vulnerable and afraid of rejection as you do. Bear it in mind when you feel unsure of yourself.
- Don't pretend to be confident and cool if inside you feel nervous. Allow others to get a little glimpse of the real you and they will warm to you.
- Develop a strategy and an action plan.
- Involve a friend and treat it as a joint project. It's a great way to keep each other motivated.
- Whenever you approach somebody new, give yourself a tangible reward, something personal and enjoyable.

CHAPTER 3

Rejection:
How to Reduce the Odds

Going over to someone you don't know takes some doing. How it turns out depends on two things:

1. How people see you
2. Your ability to read the signals the other person is sending out.

Looking friendly and confident, like someone who enjoys meeting new people, is very important because it will increase the chances of others welcoming your approach. However, the interesting thing about the second point is that this is the flip side of the same coin. Instead of focusing on how to project an attractive 'you', I'm now going to show you how you can identify some favourable clues. Clues that will help you recognise whether the other person is in the right frame of mind to be approached.

Rule number 1 is: Be observant! Yes, I know what you're thinking: 'I can't see inside people's heads so how on earth can I work out whether they're going to be interested or not?' As a matter of fact, you can. Of course I can't give you an iron-clad guarantee but I certainly can help you increase the odds in your favour.

The clues that will help you identify the people you might like to approach without too much risk of being rejected can be found in their body language, things like their posture, whether they have a friendly expression, whether they're smiling, maybe looking at you with interest in their eyes, and so on. Unless you're ultra-confident or training to become a masochist, I suggest you don't approach people who clearly signal 'Leave me alone!' by burying their nose in a newspaper or book, listening to their personal stereos, turning their body away, and crossing their arms and legs away from the crowd. All that doesn't necessarily mean that they really want to be left alone, only that if you ignore the signals you might end up disappointed.

'OK, OK!' I hear you say. 'I know all the negative signals there are to know! What I want to know is how to recognise the promising candidates! I know you mentioned being observant, but observe *what*?'

This is what to do: Don't jump straight in. Before approaching somebody, stop and look. Check if your 'quarry' is on their own or deeply engrossed in a conversation. Do they look fairly friendly and approachable or do they look as if they'd rather be left alone? There are also gestures which may not necessarily mean anything by themselves but which, when combined, send the signal that a person would like to meet either people in general or you in particular. For example, when a man sees a woman he's interested in, he will straighten his tie, stretch his body, lift his head, and stand more erect. In particular, if he feels a bit self-conscious of his real or imagined potbelly, he will try to disguise it by pushing back his shoulders and pulling his tummy in. Other things he may do – though not necessarily all at once – are to hitch up his trouser belt, adjust his cufflinks or buttons, straighten his jacket, pull his socks up if he's sitting down, or smooth his hair. All this will be followed by, or combined with, glances at the woman who caught his eye.

A woman may show her interest by, for example, playing with her hair, smoothing her dress, or quickly looking at herself in the mirror. If you notice afterwards that she's also looking at you, or doing a 'double-take', I think it's fairly safe to assume that things look promising for you.

There are times, however, when the clues are less clear. In that case you will just have to trust your instinct and take a chance, because, as you know, 'nothing ventured, nothing gained', so give it a go!

TIPS
- Be observant. Watch your 'quarry'. Is this the right time to go over to them? Do they seem to be in the right frame of mind to be approached?
- If you think the odds are in your favour, go for it. And good luck!

CHAPTER 4

Where Are All the Good Men and Women?

'That's all very well,' I hear you say, 'except that there aren't any suitable unattached people around!' If there's one complaint I keep hearing again and again from men and women alike that's the one. I guess if you're only interested in people who fall into the potential 'life-partner' category then I suppose you might be right – maybe. But I also believe that, if you only look at people you think may be 'the one!', you're being foolish and short-sighted because you will have lost the chance of meeting people who could become valuable friends. In Chapter 6, Friendship: What's It All About?, you'll see that good friends – not the 'we're just good friends' variety – are worth their weight in gold. It would, therefore, be a shame if you dismissed anybody just because the sexual chemistry doesn't strike you like a bolt of lightning.

The world is your oyster

If you're willing to keep an open mind, the world really is your oyster. There are people all around you; all you have to do is start paying attention to your surroundings wherever you happen to be. When you next go to your supermarket or your grocer's, to the bank, to a department store, bookstore, library, restaurant, or Post Office, even when you're in a queue, look around you. Start acknowledging your milkman, your postman, the garage attendant; notice the people at your place of work. There may be someone new joining your company or department, or moving into your apartment building or neighbourhood. The only exception I would make is on the grounds of safety: don't do this if it's late at night, or if there are very few people around.

I'm not suggesting, of course, that you should start staring at people. For one thing, they might think you're a little odd and, for another, we women get unnerved when we're being stared at by a stranger. The point I'm making is that we talk to many people throughout the day without even giving them a second glance, and what I'd like you to do is wake up to the possibilities.

Start noticing people, start making eye contact, start saying hello to them, or just give them a friendly nod, smile, or thank them for their help if appropriate. Believe it or not, friendliness is catching. Be friendly and more often than not people will be friendly back. Obviously, there will be times when people won't respond. Don't worry! They're probably still in shock! But even if they don't, chances are you will have cheered someone up, made someone feel good, and they will pass on those good feelings. So, stop worrying and just get on with it. I have no doubt that, one way or another, those good feelings will come right back to you.

And what's really important is that you will get into the habit of taking the initiative to be friendly. Research has come up with some unexpected results, namely that the giver of good feelings feels just as good as, if not better than, the recipient.

Another way of meeting new people is to take up new interests, especially the kinds of activities that can be shared with others. When you get used to seeing the same faces on a fairly regular basis you will find it easier to approach them.

Ideas for things to do abound. Here are a few: You could join evening classes on any subject that you're interested in, or you might like to take up sports, such as bowling or tennis or darts. Or perhaps join your local gym, the Ramblers' Club, or go hill-walking, cycling or hang-gliding – but don't start with anything too strenuous, especially if you haven't done any exercise or physical activity for a long time. Be sure to check with your doctor first.

If something less vigorous appeals to you, you might like to join a music appreciation society. Maybe you could start up a 'Friends of Mozart' or 'U2' group; you might like to try your hand at photography or watercolours. Alternatively, you could get involved in local politics, issues affecting your local community, or offer to do charity or voluntary work. Your church or synagogue probably organises socials but if they don't, why don't you suggest it and offer to help organise them. Don't forget reference libraries – where you can ask the librarian for listings of local groups, societies or clubs.

But don't just join any group for the sake of meeting new people; join because you are genuinely interested in that activity. If you have chosen one that interests and appeals to you, you know that you will have at least one thing in common with the other people there to start with – and that's even before you've met!

I don't want you to think that I underestimate the difficulties of being single in the Nineties, especially when the world seems to be populated by couples. My concern is that you should not expect to meet people just in specially designed places like parties, clubs, bars, dances or singles clubs. Someone described some of these as places where everybody knows they're there to pick somebody up or to be picked up. 'It's like a meat market,' he said. Then he added, 'It can be very demoralising.'

Since I began running my workshops, I've started asking couples where they met each other, and most of them mention the most ordinary and run-of-the-mill places, such as: their workplace, a concert, a table shared purely by chance at a restaurant, church, the bus and so on. They usually say that they just got talking, and 'one thing led to another'. Sometimes they even sound a little regretful because it doesn't seem romantic enough, even though they wouldn't change anything now. More and more people mention dating agencies, lonely hearts columns, and social dinners and seem less embarrassed to admit to using these services than they used to be – and quite rightly so.

Whenever you want to achieve something you need to have a well-rounded strategy. If you were looking for a job, you would look at advertisements, go to employment agencies and head-hunters, send speculative letters to potential employers, talk to lots of people asking for help and advice, and polish your interviewing skills. So why stick to just one method when it comes to meeting people?

Single parents

With the high rate of divorce there must be many of you out there, and you might have thought that I've forgotten all about you. I know that, for some of you, it can be particularly difficult to meet new people: little time and not much money to spare but don't despair because you have a terrific ally! Your child.

But first, let me ask you this. How do you think people meet other people? Basically, there are only two ways:

1. Directly: they meet, they like each other, they make friends and/or fall in love
2. Indirectly: they meet someone new and gradually become part of their circle of friends.

Children are great friend-makers, and they could be the key to help you make friends with other parents – remember the indirect route! Here, too, you have to take the initiative. If you're going to a park where children go to play, choose a bench where there's another parent and start chatting. Having children is a ready-made topic of conversation. But there's more: you can get involved with school activities, for example, attending PTA meetings, offering to help with the school play, becoming a school governor or perhaps organising fund-raising activities. Goodness knows schools are always in dire need of funds.

If, as a single mother, you feel isolated, then chances are that others feel just as isolated and that includes parents who stay at home looking after their children while their partners go out to work. They too could become a great source of support as well as giving you access to their own circle of friends. Most people know at least some other people, so how about organising a coffee and biscuits morning for some of your new friends and asking them to bring along one of their friends?

If you've been on your own for quite a while then you might find all this a little daunting but remember, you don't have to do everything at once. You know what they say; a journey of a thousand miles starts with that one first step. So, go on! Take it!

Dating Agencies

Dating agencies – or introduction agencies, as they prefer to be called – often provide more than a straightforward introduction service. They vary in the type of service they give, as well as in the way they operate; some offer a highly personalised service, while others merely circulate your details to their members. There are agencies that specialise in certain groups, for example, ethnic introductions such as Asian, Caribbean or Jewish; others cater for fatties, accountants (don't ask me why), or the disabled. Some specialise in professional, business, academic, creative and artistic people; or match up people on the basis of astrological compatibility, or those who are interested in green issues, personal growth, or are vegetarians. Sometimes agencies even cater for those who want to meet soulmates from other countries. Some hold parties and social events, and, finally, some don't fool around: the name of the game is marriage, not just dating.

As you can see, there's plenty to choose from, which is why

you need to do your homework to be sure you get the kind of agency and the type of service that best suit your needs. Here are some points taken from their Code of Practice to get you started:

1. Start by asking yourself: 'What kind of service am I looking for?'
2. Contact several agencies and read carefully the material they send you
3. Prepare a shortlist
4. Before you make your final choice, discuss with them your particular circumstances and be sure to ask them to tell you exactly what you can expect for your fee. Ask yourself:
   - Have they been in operation for at least two years?
   - Do they have a good local reputation? Ask around
   - Do they offer a refund guarantee?
   - Can they give you proof of their success rate? Ask them
   - How big is their database? The size is crucial: any fewer than 2,000 and you won't get much joy from them
   - Do they interview every potential member personally? That would help them weed out obviously undesirable characters
   - Do they insist on a code of conduct for the people on their books?
   - How do they protect your confidentiality?

5. As with any business that provides you with a service, especially an on-going one, make it a point to form a friendly relationship with your contact. Let them know how you're getting along with the people they introduce to you and, in particular, tell them when you're happy with the service they're providing, or when you're not. For example, are they introducing you to the kind of people you like and have things in common with? Are you having difficulties with the type of people you meet through them? Are you

unhappy because they don't introduce you to a reasonable number of people, or because the ones they do introduce to you are unsuitable? Do tell them and be as specific as you can because, unless you do, they won't be able to do anything about it.

6. While miracles can happen, don't count on it! Don't expect the impossible and, especially, don't expect them to provide you with a wonderful introduction straight away.

7. Be realistic in your expectations. This means that you should try to be clear about what's important to you. Chapter 17, How to Recognise the Right Partner for You will help you with this.

8. Be aware that there's an age range for men and women when availability is out of synch. This means that, in comparison with the demand, there are too few women under the age of 25 registered, and too few men over the age of 55. If your needs fall into this category, don't get discouraged, saying to yourself 'Why bother?', but it does mean that you should be patient. At the same time, it's just as possible to hit it lucky in your first month of membership as in your last, so don't give up!

9. Finally, bear in mind that dating agencies are just one way of meeting new people. Don't rely on them to do all the work for you.

Write to the Association of British Introduction Agencies, 25 Abingdon Road, Kensington, London W8 6AL and ask them to send you details of their members. This list is regularly updated and gives details about the kind of service they provide, how much they charge and other useful information, including the industry's Code of Practice, so that you know what you can expect from the dating agency of your choice.

Introduction agencies can be very useful as long as you don't just sit back and wait to meet your perfect match. Obviously, this can – and does – sometimes happen but there are things you can do to improve the odds in your favour, such as:

1. Be clear about what you expect the agency to do for you, and then discuss your expectations with them
2. Let the agency know how the date went and how the person matched your requirements. This is important since that's why you're parting with your hard-earned cash
3. Expect to meet a wide range of 'humanity'
4. Be open to potential friendships. Don't only hold out for the grand romance. Remember the indirect route!
5. And, finally, read this book.

Social Dinners

Another way of meeting people nowadays is at social dinners. Like everything else, they have advantages and disadvantages. The advantages are that this is a way of meeting new people in, hopefully, nice surroundings, there should be an equal number of single men and women, and you don't have to worry about what to order or who pays. Another advantage is that, if the hosts do a good job, the evening should start with drinks to give everybody the opportunity to mingle and during dinner they should ask everyone to move places with each new course thus giving you the opportunity of meeting several people in one evening and not getting stuck with one person. Of course, this advantage could turn into a disadvantage if you happen to strike it lucky and really hit it off with whoever you're sitting next to. Still, you can always exchange phone numbers and take it from there.

There are two main disadvantages I can think of: One is that some of these dinners often cost an arm and a leg, but I think it would be unreasonable to compare the price of a social dinner with that of a restaurant meal because what you're really paying for is the opportunity to meet new men and women in pleasant and safe surroundings. At the same time, the fact that everybody there can afford to pay the high fee is one of the things they have in common, and you may assume therefore that everyone has a fairly well-paying job. If it cuts deeply into your budget, I would recommend against you going to one of these dinners because not all organisers are good at running them, and you risk wasting a lot of money. Again, do your homework by asking around, talking to several organisers, reading their blurbs carefully, and talking to people who have attended their events.

The other disadvantage is that you are unlikely to meet compatible people at the first meeting. Again, this is not unreasonable. You meet all sorts of people, many of them really nice, but you don't always hit it off with every single one, and there's no reason to suppose that it would be any different with social dinners, so you may need to attend several of them before you meet someone with whom you get along well enough to want to see again.

Going to social dinners doesn't mean that that's all you need to make a success of it. By success, I mean at the very least having a good time. Whether or not the evening turns out all right is truly in your own hands, and this means keeping an open mind, expecting only to have an enjoyable time and to meet pleasant people. And, who knows? You might, unexpectedly, come away with a new friend or a new love.

Lonely Hearts Columns

With lonely hearts columns you can play it one of two ways:

1. You can reply to the ads
2. You can insert your own.

My own inclination is to insert your own, using a box number for safety reasons. You don't want the world to know that you're on your own and where you live, and this is even more important if you're a woman. If you insert your own ad you're more in control, but the hardest part is to draft it in a way that does you justice. Try not to sound like every other ad on the page. If you go through them you'll notice that sometimes there's little to choose between them even though the people involved are vastly different from one another.

You're bound to get a reasonable level of response and it's much easier to form an opinion from letters than from little classified ads. Also, it's up to you to decide which you want to follow up.

A word of caution for you women out there: whenever you arrange to meet a new man, even if it is at a public place which, I hope, goes without saying, do ask for his phone number and give it to a friend of yours as a safety precaution before you go out to meet him. If he is reluctant to give it to you, say that you need it in case you're delayed for some reason or something comes up and you need to postpone. I wish such warnings weren't necessary but I guess it's a reflection of an increasingly uncertain world. Engage your brain, use your common sense and then go out and enjoy yourself!

Remember, meeting people is a bit like throwing a stone in a pond – it causes lots and lots of ripples. And it's the same every time you meet somebody new. You never know what will happen. You might just have a pleasant chat or even an enjoyable evening, or they may become a friendly but casual acquaintance, a chum or a lover. They may introduce you to their circle of friends or they may not. In the beginning you won't know who will become what, but the point is things can only happen when you start meeting people. Without that, there's nothing. When you meet someone who takes your fancy *and* you've read this book, you'll know what to do.

TIPS

- There are people all around you. Open your eyes, open your mind, and open your heart to the possibility of love and friendship.

- Start paying attention to people, acknowledging them, saying hello and giving them a friendly nod or smile. But don't stare! It can be very unnerving!
- Change your routine and take up new interests.
- Investigate new alternatives for meeting people such as introduction agencies, lonely hearts columns and social dinners.
- Always ensure you take sensible safety precautions.
- Read this book and have fun!

CHAPTER 5

Getting Relationships Off the Ground

Making friends or forming any kind of relationship happens only gradually and covers three distinct stages:

Stage 1: First impressions

We start every new encounter by forming 'first impressions' of one another. This generally happens when we see each other either – as the poets put it – across a crowded room or, more casually, when someone new moves into our neighbourhood, or joins our department at work. It may also happen when we see someone on a fairly regular basis at the launderette or the supermarket, socially in our leisure time, at business events, or simply in our day-to-day life.

Friendships and relationships tend to develop where there are opportunities for frequent contact, for example, if we live near each other, work in the same office, go to the same club or meeting place because the more opportunities there are to exchange a smile and a few words, the better the chances of getting to know and, perhaps, like one another. If we often meet when enjoying a mutual interest such as ballroom dancing, a weekly drawing class, or music appreciation outings we know that we have at least one thing in common before we even speak to each other.

Stage 2: 'Growing' the relationship

This is a very important stage because now we're moving from accidentally bumping into each other to seeking someone out deliberately and arranging to meet for a drink or a meal – a clear signal that we would like to get to know them better. To move from Stage 1 to Stage 2 it's useful to know how to suggest that first date, and if you're worried about this, help is at hand in Chapter 12, Why Do Men . . .? Why Do Women . . .? Questions and Answers.

You may stay in Stage 2 for quite a while, spending the first few meetings talking over a drink or a meal. This is where you begin to exchange information and to 'self-disclose', as we call it in the trade. Self-disclosing is an art in itself and there is more detailed information about how to go about it in Chapter 18, What Do You say After You Say 'Hello'?

Studies have shown that we tend to like people with whom we have things in common, who are similar to us in terms of background, interests, beliefs, general attitudes and values. So, whether or not we move on to Stage 3 depends on two things:

1. How much we have in common
2. How good we feel when we are together.

'Rewards' is the jargon for the 'feel good' factor which comes about when we are with people who are generally warm and friendly, fun to be with, cheerful, interesting and enjoyable. And, best of all, when they act as if they really liked us and are interested in us. This is one of the factors that enables us to decide whether we want to move on to Stage 3 which is why making *them* feel interesting and attractive is such an important social skill.

One of the things that distinguishes this stage from the next one is that here we're both likely to be on our best behaviour. We're trying to impress each other, trying to avoid saying or doing anything that might make them think less of us and 'spoil' things. We make more of an effort than usual, taking extra care with our appearance or, if we invite them home, tidy up – or hide everything under the bed so it looks tidy – and generally mind our Ps and Qs. And the reason we do this, of course, is that we want them to think that we're attractive and likeable. All this is understandable but somewhat risky and I will expand on this in Chapter 10, What Attracts People to One Another.

Stage 3: 'Cementing' the relationship

This is a major step forward in the friendship or love relationship, and happens when we decide to meet regularly, for example, to have lunch every Wednesday, or to play squash once a week. That's when we start having deeper heart-to-heart conversations, trusting one another with much more personal information. We begin to look forward to seeing each other, start caring if they're feeling good, down or upset, and develop mutual affection or love.

How long each stage – and each step within each stage – takes is impossible to say. You might as well ask 'How long is a piece of string?' How long it takes depends on various factors such as whether you're impulsive or reserved, whether you 'click' straight away or where you are in your life. For example, if you have just finished a relationship, you might still feel too bruised to let yourself become attracted to someone new or, if you're very involved in your career, you may feel there's no 'space' for a love relationship right now, although you might welcome a new friendship.

If you're curious about the whole process, you might like to do a little exercise that will help you get a sense of how long things took to develop in your previous relationships:

Exercise

Think back to one or two love relationships, preferably ones that were medium- or long-term. Now think of one or two close chums, either of the same or of the opposite sex. Taking each person in turn, go through the process described below. Start by thinking back to the time when you met for the first time and ask yourself the following questions under the various headings:

1. FIRST MEETING
   How did you meet? Was it at one of those one-off social occasions like a concert or a party, at a wine bar or a pub? Or did you bump into each other every once in a while, for instance in the office, at evening classes, the gym, the church or synagogue, or at choir practice before you actually met? How long did you stay in the 'Fancy meeting you here!' or 'Hello again!' stage before arranging to meet somewhere? Or, if you met at a one-off occasion, how long was it until one phoned the other to arrange to meet?

2. FIRST 'REAL' MEETING AND 'GROWING' THE RELATIONSHIP
   How long did this initial 'getting-to-know-you' period last? How long until you started noticing how much you enjoy their company and that the feeling was probably mutual? How long did it take you to realise that you've begun to look forward to seeing them again?

3. 'CEMENTING' THE RELATIONSHIP
   How long was it until you decided to meet regularly, say once a week or more, and do things together? How long before you noticed that you started phoning each other just to have a chat? How long until you realised that you're both sharing fairly intimate and personal things? How long until you discovered that you cared for each other, either in a platonic, affectionate way or that you began to feel sexually attracted to them?

These are some indications about how you like your relationships – either acquaintances or romantic attachments or anything in-between – to grow. But they're just that, clues. We all change, learning from previous experiences – or not, as the case may be. We may have decided to be a little more cautious and less impulsive in future, or that people are OK after all and, provided we take certain precautions, we now feel a little more comfortable about taking a few more risks – such as taking the initiative.

In the next chapter, I will talk about the mysteries of friendship, what makes them and what breaks them. In the one after that, I will explore the secrets of love. I expect you may well find one or two surprises in both these chapters.

CHAPTER 6

Friendship:
What's It All About?

It seems to me that the word 'friendship' has been devalued. We tend to call our most casual acquaintances 'friends' or, when we are trying to discourage somebody's romantic aspirations, we tell them 'let's just be friends', when what we really mean is that we don't want to go to bed with them.

The truth is that to have even one or two close friends is to be rich beyond measure. Friends stay when lovers have long gone. They're there, holding our hand, cursing the faithless lover for having hurt us, continuing to love us even when we behave badly and always being there when we need them – through the laughter and the tears. And no, I'm not exaggerating.

Studies have shown that lack of friendships can often make people feel lonely and isolated and, unless they have a fulfilling love relationship, they find it harder to deal with life's ups and downs. The same studies have identified the specific social skills that such people lack causing them to have difficulty establishing the kind of friendships they would dearly like to have.

But, before I go into detail about what you need to do to 'grow' your friendships, let's look at some general principles:

- Probably the most important piece of advice I can give you is, first and foremost, work on developing your self-esteem. A healthy self-esteem is absolutely critical, both for friendships and for love relationships. A good start is to read Chapter 24, How to Care for Yourself: The Magic of Self-Esteem and there are many good books available on the subject.

- Don't assume that you can't change or learn new ways of doing things. Sometimes all you need are new ideas, new skills and a new strategy, a new approach for meeting people.
- Don't give up even if at first you feel anxious or if people don't instantly welcome you with open arms. Your success rate will grow as you gradually become more confident, I promise.
- Learn to trust people in general. Even if someone lets you down, remember that it was just one person and not the whole human race. If you don't trust others they won't be able to warm to you and you will get stuck in a negative cycle.
- Lighten up. Don't take yourself too seriously. A good start is to try to forget about how nervous you are and to focus instead on the other person – who is probably just as nervous.
- To have friends you need to *be* a friend. This may sound like a truism, but many people don't know what that actually means, believing it is simply something to do with feeling warmth, liking and affection for somebody. In fact what makes a relationship – any relationship – work is less what you feel and more what you do. The old saying 'Actions speak louder than words' is particularly true with relationships.

To make friends you need to:

- Take the initiative in approaching people.
- Let people get to know you. Start by telling them a little about yourself, then gradually open up a little more.

- Show that you're genuinely interested in the other person by asking them questions, really listening to their replies, and then picking up on some of their comments to keep the conversation flowing. Both this skill and the one above are described in Chapter 18, What Do You Say After You Say 'Hello'?

- Learn to show them that you like them and enjoy their company. Others have a deep need to know that, just as you and I do. You can do this without saying a word, just by having a friendly expression (you can practise different faces in front of a mirror), looking them in the eye, smiling and using a tone of voice that reflects friendliness. You can also do it by using words and this is explored in more detail in Chapter 20, In Praise of Praise.

But to develop and maintain friendships you need to observe certain rules. You may never have thought of relationships having rules, but in fact, they all do. Some things, such as jobs, video hire or marriage have written contracts; social relationships, such as friendships or dating, for example, have unwritten ones. The problem with unwritten rules is that, because they are usually not discussed, each of you may assume that the other has the same set of rules in mind and that you both regard the same things as important. And that can lead to trouble!

The interesting thing about these rules — even though the word seems to have a bit of a punishing feel to it, doesn't it? — is that they make people feel good about being together, particularly the positive ones, the do's as opposed to the don'ts. Rules about what should or should not be done to keep the relationship satisfying for both parties can make it positively rewarding. People who are popular are rewarding to be with and that applies both to friendship and romance.

Below is a set of rules, a list of the actions and behaviour that people expect from their friends. This is based on responses by large numbers of people in studies carried out by Dr Michael Argyle. You will probably find some too obvious to mention; others you may find less obvious. In no particular order of importance, friends:

- look at each other in the eye while talking together
- engage in gentle teasing and light-hearted banter, laughing together and touching (see Chapter 21, The Power of Touch and Chapter 26, Laughter: The Missing Link)
- are emotionally supportive, willing to listen, offering and accepting encouragement and advice
- show unconditional approval and appreciation
- show affection
- tune into the other's mood, either trying to cheer them up or simply listening to them, whatever the friend happens to need at that particular time
- are understanding, tolerant and considerate of the other's personal problems
- are aware when the other is having a difficult time and give them a call
- share news of successes
- share problems and disappointments
- trust the other with their personal thoughts, feelings and opinions, and discuss intimate topics
- volunteer help in time of need
- repay debts and favours
- remember birthdays and other special occasions (Men: take note as this is particularly important to women)
- keep promises, however small
- stand up for them, if they are criticised behind their back
- respect their privacy
- are tolerant of other friendships
- keep confidences
- are not jealous if the friend happens to meet someone special and fall in love.

On the other hand, friends don't:

- nag or criticise
- make passes at a friend's partner
- put them down in front of others.

Obviously, these rules are general and you may come up with other things that are also important to you but that have not been mentioned on the list. That's fine.

Some of these rules are more important than others and the weight you give to each of them depends on you and your friend. But be aware of them, because they will help you form mutually satisfying friendships and that will bring you one major step closer to having an even happier and more fulfilling life.

Although the list may seem long and complicated, it can be summed up very simply. We like to make friends with people who are warm and friendly, cheerful, interesting, kind and helpful and, above all, people who like us and show that they're interested in us. If, on the other hand, we behave in such a way that our friends feel that we don't respect or appreciate them, abuse their trust and can't be counted on in time of need, then we shouldn't be too surprised if the friendship breaks up or fizzles out.

OK, now you know the rules. Is this really all there is to it? Well, I wish I could say 'yes' – but I can't. Other things can and do get in the way. For example, people who are not very good at making friends make three major mistakes:

1. They don't pay enough attention to the other person's signals
2. They misinterpret them
3. They make false assumptions about the people they meet.

Mistakes people make

1. We assume that the person will behave in the same way in other situations as they do wherever we normally see them.

2. We assume that, if that person has one or two good qualities, they don't have any negative ones. We are reluctant to accept that someone can be both generous and untidy, fun and unreliable, affectionate and forgetful, and so on.
3. We tend to be influenced too much by first impressions and make assumptions about what kind of people they are with little evidence one way or another.
4. When we discover one or two things we have in common, we assume we have more in common than we might actually have.
5. When we discover one or two things we don't like about a person, we assume they have no positive qualities that we might truly value and appreciate. This often makes us miss out on potentially rewarding relationships.

OK, now you have quite a bit of inside information. Surely there can't be more? Well, yes there is. And you will find it fascinating, I'm sure. It's all about Love (with a capital 'L'), which is the topic of my next chapter.

TIPS
- Rule No. 1: Develop your self-esteem. People who like and accept themselves make better friends.
- Experiment with new ideas, skills and approaches to discover which work best for you.
- Most people are kind and friendly. Learn to trust them; otherwise you'll keep them at arm's length and you will only sabotage your own efforts.
- Don't take yourself too seriously. Lighten up!
- Become the kind of friend you would like to have for yourself.
- Re-read the action list for making friends.
- Re-read how you can create rewarding friendships. The long list boils down to being warm and friendly, cheerful,

interesting, kind and helpful. It also includes showing that you like them and that you're interested in them.

- Remember: people are a mixture of attractive and irritating qualities. That's what's so wonderful about them.
- Remember, too, that people are not robots: they can be unpredictable.
- Don't make up your mind about a person too soon, one way or another.
- And finally, never give up! If you persist, you will develop an even more rewarding life.

CHAPTER 7

Love:
An Insider's Guide

Not only is friendship different from love – which you always knew – but (and not everybody knows this) love comes in various guises. And that's why couples often get into dead-end arguments like 'You don't really love me!' 'Oh yes! I do!' – 'Oh no! You don't! If you did, you wouldn't want to spend your free time with your grotty friends or watching the telly. You'd want to make love ten times a day, you would share your innermost secrets', and on and on, and on and on . . .

Research has identified three separate ingredients that make up this thing called love:

1. Passion
2. Intimacy
3. Commitment

and, not only do they grow at different rates, but they can combine in many different ways. This is why, while both partners know they love the other, they sometimes don't feel loved in return.

1. Passion
Passion can grow in two different ways. One happens when you feel as if you've been struck by lightning. Most people call this 'love at first sight' though I prefer to call it 'lust at first sight'. I know, I know – I can already hear howls of outrage

and I bet I'll be inundated with letters about how you knew the moment you laid eyes on him – or her – that he – or she – was *the one*.

The other way passion develops is over a period of time. As you begin to like and to become more and more drawn to one another, you'll start feeling more and more sexually attracted. There will always be exceptions but usually trust and closeness take time to develop, however boring this may sound.

In the beginning you will find that you can hardly keep your hands off each other, but as the relationship develops the quality of the passion gradually changes along with the relationship itself. What happens is that passion tends to level off when you become used to one another. But if it combines with the intimacy and commitment that come as you become more attuned with each other, growing together at all levels – emotionally, mentally and spiritually – you're going to want each other all the more. That's why people say that sex starts, not in, but out of bed. If you let yourself become too busy to spend time with one another, enjoying yourselves and having a good time, then the passion will simply evaporate. On the other hand, if you both make sure you do things to avoid getting into a sexual rut, your love-making will continue to be fulfilling.

2. Intimacy

As you start feeling more comfortable with each other, you begin to explore the similarities and differences between the two of you, confiding in each other your innermost thoughts and feelings. This implies trust and the willingness to take a risk by making yourself vulnerable to each other because the pre-condition of intimacy is that you show yourself as you really are. That can be really scary. On the one hand, you truly yearn for this kind of closeness but, on the other, you often hold back wondering 'How will he – or she – react?', 'Will he – or she – hold it against me?', 'Use it against me in some way?', 'Tell someone else?', 'Will he – or she – still like me?' And yet, when you take the risk in spite of the anxiety and find complete acceptance, you experience a rush of emotion and an increase in your feelings of love. I promise you, there is nothing in the whole world like being truly accepted by the person you care for.

When you enter a new relationship and you have things in common, intimacy tends to grow quite fast at first because you're just dying to know everything there is to know about the other. Then, after a while, as you become more and more familiar with each other, this slows down until it finally levels off.

By now you know that I'm a firm believer in the old adage 'Actions speak louder than words' so, are there any other clues that indicate you're developing a genuine closeness? You're highly likely to be well on your way when you want what's best for your partner (irrespective of whether or not it's best for you too), when you feel happy when you're together, knowing – preferably from past experience – that you can count on them when in need, when you both feel truly understood by the other, when you're generous with both time and money, when you give and receive emotional support, when you feel glad your partner is in your life, and when you naturally and frequently enjoy intimate conversations with each other. This last one is what most people think of when they talk of intimacy.

Sharing is a critical part of the closeness and intimacy that develops in a happy long-term relationship but this includes other things too. Intimacy also means continuing to share similar interests and activities, exchanging ideas, laughing together, discussing things calmly and getting involved in joint projects of whatever kind. The more things you enjoy doing together and the more often you do them, the more lovingly you're likely to think of each other and, therefore, behave towards each other. This way of being together, which is called in jargon, 'cohesion', also has the important side-effect of helping you as a couple to handle your day-to-day stresses and conflicts in a much more constructive and helpful way.

The main danger to intimacy is reaching a point where you believe you know each other so well that you start making assumptions and to take each other for granted. However, having read Chapter 1, What Do People Want?, I expect you already know how to side-step this potential minefield.

There's another danger to intimacy which can come about in two ways:

1. You may stop confiding your worries in your partner (or your partner in you) in the mistaken belief that you're protecting the other. The intention may be kind but you or your partner will feel left out and kept at arm's length. And that's when the relationship begins to suffer.
2. One or both of you may revert to your normal way of behaving once the novelty wears off. You may go back to being reserved and keeping yourself to yourself as you used to; or one of you may want to share everything but the other just doesn't want to know.

Either way, in the end you become distant and keep growing further and further apart.

What I'm talking about are your individual beliefs and styles of communication and this is something you may be able to find out early on in the relationship before things really hot up, but first you need to be clear about how you yourself prefer – or need – to communicate. And not just in the beginning but throughout the life of the relationship. Working through the questions in Chapter 17, How to Recognise the Right Partner for You is a good way to start.

3. Commitment

This is something else altogether. Again, people – and this probably applies especially to men – often don't realise that the word commitment means more than just commitment to getting married or moving in together.

Commitment goes through a series of stages. The first one is when you decide that you want to stop going out with other people and date each other exclusively. The next stage happens when you realise that this is the person you want to spend the rest of your life with.

But this is not, as most people tend to believe, the end of it. In fact, commitment involves sticking up for each other, staying together through thick and thin, throughout good times and bad, continuing to support and encourage each other, and showing each other that your relationship comes first, now and always. This is one of the things I mean when I talk about working at the relationship. Commitment always starts very low and, at first, tends to grow slowly and then, gradually, faster until it stays fairly stable, unless things happen that make the couple review just how committed is committed.

Passion, intimacy and commitment grow at different rates and they are each affected by different things that are responsible for whether or not the relationship continues to grow, remains stable or fades away.

Falling head over heels in love is something everybody should experience at least once in their lifetime. Unfortunately – or fortunately, if we want to be able to function properly again in the real world – this stage doesn't last long. And, in fact, this is the worst possible time to make a decision to move in together or get married. The reason for this is that the early stage of love is an all-consuming obsession that takes up all our energies, giving us time to think of little else but yearn to be with the object of our passion, whom we have put on a pedestal. They are absolutely perfect: a god or a goddess. Nothing less. I know what you're thinking: I bet you know dozens of examples of people who met in the morning, got engaged in the afternoon and married that very evening – and, fifty years later, they're still together and passionately in love. To be honest, I agree with you, because I can quote the example of my own parents – actually it took them six months to tie the knot, but the principle still applies.

However, there are very good reasons why you shouldn't count on this nowadays. For one thing, society has changed dramatically. The often unrealistic as well as unspoken expectations we place on our partner can – and often do – break a promising relationship. For more on how this can happen, see Chapter 8, Expectations: They Can Make Your Relationships Fail! Having said that, I can still offer you hope. In a number of recent studies, results showed that the amount of passion as well as companionlike love can remain fairly high, declining only slowly over the years. Later in this chapter I will list the things that happily married couples do that keep their relationship alive and vibrant for many, many years.

Love goes through three predictable stages and you stand a better chance of making it last if you work your way through all the stages to establish whether you can live with this person through thick and thin. These stages are:

1. Initial excitement
2. Disillusionment, or seeing the real person rather than the fantasy
3. Accepting the person as they really are and making the final commitment.

How do love relationships grow?

How do we progress from falling in love to a more stable and long-term emotional attachment? The sequence follows casual dating, where you also continue seeing other people, through to more serious dating, where you start going out only with each other, all the way to engagement, moving in together or getting married.

As you progress through this sequence, the nature of your relationship undergoes various changes:

1. You start spending more and more time in each other's company.
2. You get together in different situations, doing different things, with different people, such as your friends and or your family and theirs.
3. You gradually like each other more and feel more love and trust.
4. You start expressing both more positive and more negative feelings towards each other. By this time you're feeling increasingly committed to the other person, but it's a bit like two hedgehogs trying to move past each other avoiding the spines – carefully, yet sometimes accidentally bumping into each other's tender spots.
5. You become increasingly concerned about the other's welfare; you're happy when they're happy – and sad when they're sad.
6. You start being more open about the more private aspects of yourself, including more deeply held personal beliefs, thoughts and feelings about yourself, your partner and the relationship itself.
7. You both begin to see yourselves as an 'item' and your friends start treating you as a twosome. At the same time you both feel less uncertain about where you're going as a couple.

There are four types of feelings that characterise the growth of a relationship:

A. *Love*, i.e. affection, caring, feelings of closeness and inter-dependence.
B. *Conflict and negative feelings*, i.e. arguments, disagreements and problems.

Many people are a little frightened of conflict, so you may be surprised and relieved to hear that one important thing researchers have found is that love and conflict not only are not mutually exclusive but, more than that, conflict has been shown to have a beneficial impact on the maintenance of the relationship and increased closeness and intimacy.

This, obviously, needs some explanation. First of all, every relationship that involves intense emotions and where the couple lives together is bound to have disagreements. That's perfectly healthy even in the happiest of relationships. However, many couples believe that there is no room for conflict in happy relationships. And that's why they suppress their negative feelings and settle for a life that on the surface seems smooth and peaceful. But what people often don't realise is that suppressing one kind of feeling, such as anger or resentment, unintentionally and unexpectedly also deadens other emotions, such as passion. Eventually, the couple become distanced from one another because there is a very important part of their relationship that they pretend doesn't exist and, therefore, cannot resolve.

C. *Ambivalence*, i.e. uncertainty or confusion about your feelings for the other person plus anxiety about losing your independence or your readiness for commitment, either in general or to that person in particular.

D. *Maintenance*, when you both discuss your relationship, talk about your feelings and needs, and try to change each other's behaviour to make it easier to come together in relative harmony.

Rules

As with friendships, love relationships also have rules. When researchers interviewed people about the rules that apply in the dating stages, interestingly, most of the general rules they came up with were the same as for developing and keeping friendships. However, not surprisingly, love involves additional rules as well, such as:

- Being punctual. This is important because it shows interest and consideration
- Showing an interest in each other's daily activities
- Surprising each other with little gifts. This shows that you're thinking of the other even when you're not together
- Showing that you are sexually attracted to them
- Touching the other person intentionally and affectionately (for more on this, read Chapter 21, The Power of Touch)
- Being faithful to one another.

The reason these rules are also particularly important in a committed love relationship is because couples tend to spend a lot of time together, especially if they're married or living together. Also, compared with friendships, the emotional involvement is considerably more intense, there are more possibilities for hurting the other and for disagreements. Like in every other area of your lives, without signposts you get lost. So, the idea behind the rules is to help you not only maintain the relationship but also make it as mutually fulfilling as possible. Otherwise the costs will be too high and either one of you may decide to bail out.

Why relationships break down
What causes love relationships to break down? As you can see, there are all sorts of reasons apart from going off each other, such as:

- Moving away either to study or in pursuit of a career opportunity
- Going off each other

- Meeting someone else
- Parental disapproval
- Friends' disapproval
- One or the other feels too dependent or stifled
- One loves more than the other so the relationships feels unequal
- In the case of newly single people with children, the children have often been found to create conflicts of interest and loyalties. On top of that, there are also the financial pressures that come from having to support two families and that often causes rows and resentment
- The costs are higher than the rewards.

The rewards have already been examined in some detail but, under costs, people include all sorts of things such as giving up doing something else, or not seeing their friends as often as they used to, the cost of going out, not feeling appreciated, constant rowing, not having sex, and anything that makes them feel bad, lonely or otherwise deprived in some way. The tragedy is that so many people have no idea what they are doing wrong so they can't put it right; but you're one of the lucky ones because in later chapters you will learn the skills that will enable you both to start and to keep fulfilling relationships.

On a more positive note, studies have also found that, where the relationship is on the whole mutually fulfilling, the partners are more willing and able to try to find a solution by discussing the situation, listening to each other, and taking each other's feelings into account. On the other hand, couples whose relationship is unsatisfactory tend to keep their heads down, hoping that things will improve by themselves, or they may start having affairs or even leave altogether.

I will finish this chapter by giving you the secrets that keep so many couples deeply in love for many, many years, even allowing for setbacks, conflicts and arguments, and that enable them to safeguard the essential core of their love. So what is the magic recipe?

Love behaviours of happily married couples

1. *They express their love verbally.* They say 'I love you' to each other – or words to that effect (in contrast to that attitude best summarised by 'What do you mean, do I love you? I married you, didn't I?').

2. *They are physically affectionate.* This includes hand-holding, hugging, kissing, cuddling and comforting. It also means getting each other a cup of tea or coffee without waiting to be asked, or a pillow, or anything you know will make the other one more comfortable.

3. *They express their love sexually.* People who are happily in love regard sexual intimacy as an important way of expressing their love. This doesn't mean that they regard sex as the most important thing in their relationships, and there's a dramatic difference in the frequency of love-making among happily married couples. But for them sex is another way of expressing their love and caring, and they invest deep emotional feelings in their love-making.

4. *They express their appreciation and admiration for each other.* Happy couples talk about what they like, enjoy and admire in each other. As a result both partners feel appreciated and valued. Each comments on things such as the way the other looks or something the other did. The point is that they notice and comment, expressing their pride in each other.

5. *They disclose intimate information about themselves.* They have a willingness to share more of themselves with their partner than with any other person. They share their thoughts, feelings, hopes, dreams, aspirations, hurts, anger, longings, and memories of painful or embarrassing experiences. And they're truly interested in what makes their partner tick. Of course, sometimes one partner finds it easier

to talk about such things than the other but both reach out to each other, trust one another above anyone else and truly listen to their partner.

6. *They are each other's emotional support system.* They are each other's best friend, always there for each other in times of illness, difficulty, hardship and crisis. They are helpful, nurturing and devoted to each other and to each other's interests and well-being.

   In happy marriages both partners recognise the importance of doing this whereas more usually it's the woman who does it at the expense of her own needs. Also, they both recognise that mature and equal loving relationships are those where neither partner drains or exploits the other either intentionally or unintentionally but where both nurture and are nurtured.

7. *They express their love materially.* They express their affection with gifts – small or large, it doesn't matter – and they do so for special reasons or for no reason at all. Under this heading also comes doing things to make life easier for their partner, like occasionally taking on the other's responsibilities and tasks, and doing more than their agreed share of the work.

8. *They accept demands or put up with shortcomings.* They recognise that demands and shortcomings are part of every happy relationship and they respond with compassion, tolerance and grace. They don't anguish over the other's imperfections nor do they try to change them. To repeat the analogy I mentioned in an earlier chapter, they hear the music instead of the coughing.

9. *They make time to be alone together.* This is time to be spent exclusively with each other, doing things together that they both enjoy, and generally having a good time. If they have to choose between outside demands and the needs of their relationship, they will usually choose to be together unless they're convinced that there's a very good reason for

doing otherwise. This in no way detracts from their individuality; what it does is highlight the fact that their times together are precious.

The bottom line is that once these couples have decided that their love really matters to them at least as much as their work, and their leisure and social activities, and that having a successful relationship is just as important as having a successful career, then they *do* find the time to be together. They know it's now or never.

TIPS
- Put into practice the rules that govern love relationships and friendships. This will enable you to nurture relationships that are mutually rewarding.
- Be aware of the costs in relationships so you can keep them under control wherever possible.
- Do as the most successful couples do:
  Express your love verbally by telling your partner you love them – and telling them often.
  Be physically affectionate. For many people, especially women, cuddling and touching is as important as talking and making love.
  Express your love sexually. Frequency is not the issue, it's the emotion you invest in it that counts.
  Express your appreciation and admiration for each other.
  Share intimate information about yourselves.
  Accept that, like you, no one is perfect. Be tolerant and compassionate.
  Make time to be alone together.
  Be your partner's emotional support system.
  Buy them little gifts for no reason at all and occasionally do more than your fair share of the chores.
- Remember, when it comes to your relationship, today is all you've got.

CHAPTER 8

Expectations: They Can Make Your Relationships Fail!

Let's talk about expectations. First of all, what are they? Expectations are usually an unspoken set of beliefs, covering all sorts of different areas, about how men and women, or husbands and wives, should behave. What makes most of them so treacherous is the fact that they're often also unconscious, and the reason they're so damaging is because they discount individual differences.

However, not all expectations are damaging. There are many positive ones that can actually strengthen our relationships, for example, 'Partners should be able to take it in turns to be strong or vulnerable,' 'Partners should be generally supportive and share in the decision-making – including me', 'Partners should bring to the relationship their strengths and talents, irrespective of whether they're a man or a woman'. These kinds of expectations allow both of us to be flexible, to do the best we can, to open ourselves up to new possibilities and experiences, and to let go of resentments. People with these kinds of expectations have learned to like themselves, and to be generally more compassionate and tolerant. And, best of all, they don't expect either themselves or their partner to live up to unrealistic or stereotyped expectations.

Many of us, though, are still burdened with rigid, conventional and outdated expectations. One way to identify them is when you hear your partner – or yourself – preface the word 'should' with words like 'you' or 'they', therefore imposing a set of beliefs – yours – on to others. Let me give you an example. A woman expects that men *should* be confident and strong. Stereotypical expectations such as this one usually have deeper underlying beliefs and fears. In this case, the fear is likely to be that, if her partner is not confident and strong, he won't be able to look after her and, if he can't look after her, then what's going to become of her?

Such negative and stereotypical expectations based on the roles of men and women, and husbands and wives, have major consequences that will affect you, your partner and your relationship. For example, let's use the scenario just described, starting with how it would affect the woman. If she expects her partner to be strong for her, what she would be doing is giving up her own strength. Eventually she would become unable to look after herself, even if circumstances should make it necessary.

In her partner's case, he will be forced to play a false role because no one can be confident and strong all of the time. That means that he won't be able to live up to her unrealistic expectations and demands, she will end up resenting him and he, in turn, will end up resenting her for expecting him to be super-human. He will feel he's in a no-win situation – and he will be right!

I don't think I need to draw you a map of how this would affect your relationship. In fact, the one thing that expectations do is set you up – and your partner – for disappointment. Here's a very brief list of examples, just as a sampler:

- 'It's the man's place to pursue the woman'
- 'Men should be the ones to change electrical plugs and women to do the laundry'
- 'Men should be confident and strong; I can't respect a man who shows he's unsure of himself'
- 'When you go out on a date, the man should pay'
- 'The husband's career always comes first'
- 'Career women are real ball-breakers'

- 'Men are adulterous; that's their nature'
- 'Men are always ready for sex'
- 'Husbands should remain romantic and attentive, like my Dad used to be with my Mum'
- 'If he loved me, he would know what I want without my having to spell it out'
- 'If he forgets my birthday, he doesn't really love me'
- 'If he really loved me, he would not want to go out with his friends'
- 'If I have to ask for what I want, it doesn't really count'
- 'If a couple really love each other, the marriage will work (*This is the biggest and most dangerous of all expectations!*).

How expectations can trip you up

Let me show you how expectations can set you up only to let you down, by giving you a few examples together with a few ideas for dealing with them. Some of these examples are relatively trivial, but others are very serious and can virtually destroy what could be a very promising romance. Let's start with a relatively minor expectation – and the reason I say it's minor, is that most people go through it and reach the other side safely, although probably shaken and more than a little stirred.

EXAMPLE 1

Here we are, head over heels in love. We spend a little time together and feel wonderful when we do. So we start spending more time together and we feel even more wonderful. It's as if we're walking on air or touching heaven with our hands. Surely this feeling will last forever?

Before long we spend all our free time together and that's when we begin to notice little things here and there – things we hadn't noticed before. Maybe she had this habit when you first met, but then you thought that it was so cute! Now, for no apparent reason, you find it irritating. Or you loved the way he seemed to be the strong and silent type. Somehow that made you feel cherished and protected. Now he just seems moody – period. Or you're suddenly aware that she seems a teensy weensy bit needy and clingy, something you hadn't realised before. Or you now notice that he doesn't phone when he said he would, and that she's beginning to sound like a nag.

What on earth is happening? Did we expect too much? Was it all an illusion? Maybe it wasn't the 'real thing' after all? Well, the answer is yes, yes, and perhaps. Yes, we did expect too much; yes, it was an illusion; but perhaps it is the real thing after all.

Illusions happen when we put people on a pedestal and then find that they have feet of clay. They're neither Prince Charming nor a wonderful Princess after all. That doesn't mean that they're necessarily a frog or an old witch. It wasn't their fault. It was ours for indulging in unrealistic fantasies and expectations. If you remember, this is the second stage in a developing romance. The scales fall from our eyes and we see the object of our passion or dreams as they really are – a human being with a combination of both lovable and irritating qualities, just like us.

Yes, it can be momentarily disappointing but there is something you can do to protect yourself in the future, and I hope I'm in time to prevent you from falling into the same trap again. All you have to do is:

BE AWARE THAT PERFECTION IS AN ILLUSION AND THAT THERE'S NO SUCH THING AS THE 'PERFECT PARTNER'. YOU ARE NOT, NOR IS ANYBODY ELSE.

EXAMPLE 2

This expectation is one that's usually held by women. When you were seeing each other once a week, he would tell you how good he felt when you were together, so you expected that he would feel twice as good now that you meet twice a week.

Instead, he's saying that he wants to go and play golf (or darts) with his mates.

This particular expectation of yours that just because you're in love you should spend all your free time together is a little more serious because it can lead to resentment. Surely, what you want is for him to want to be with you gladly and not because you expect it. So if, for example, you're aware from the very beginning that he enjoys a weekly game of squash or that she enjoys going out with her friends, then I suggest not only that you'd be wise to expect it to continue, but that you actively encourage it. If you do so they will look forward to being with you again. Although you often find it hard to admit it, the real issue is fear – fear that your partner will leave you. But the reality is that the tighter you try to tie someone to you, the harder they will strive to get away. Let them go and they will come back. Besides, if you don't, it will only result in resentment once the novelty of the relationship has worn off.

EXAMPLE 3

This next disappointed expectation is another one that tends to happen mostly to women and often comes to light after you get married or move in together. One day you notice that he has stopped taking you out for dinner or dancing, or buying you flowers or chocolates. That's when you start to feel taken for granted. (A small aside here: I have a suspicion that not being bought flowers or boxes of chocolates or even going out dancing any more is not the real reason why you feel taken for granted. After all, you're no longer courting. What I think is happening is that you no longer feel special or visible. You're stuck in a routine and you probably have begun to feel as if you're part of the furniture or the wallpaper, and that your partner doesn't seem to notice you're there any more. You don't talk as you used to, you certainly don't feel listened to, and you no longer spend time together having fun.)

Even if this is happening, all is still not lost. There are a number of things you can do. First of all, instead of sitting back, feeling hard done by, complaining and hoping he will change (he won't) try taking the initiative.

1. First, why don't you, for example, book a restaurant and invite him out. But face the possibility that he may have made other plans. After all, you didn't check with him in advance because that would have spoiled the surprise. If this happens, then yes, of course it's OK to feel disappointed but, whatever else you do, don't make an issue out of it and certainly don't expect him to change his plans. The point will have been made – and you can still use your reservation with a girlfriend, if you wish. However, now that the cat is out of the bag, arrange a convenient date for the two of you and book again.

2. The second thing you can do is take the opportunity to start making the kinds of changes you would like your partner to make. Prepare a special meal, buy a bottle of good wine (though even plonk will do – it's the thought that counts!) and encourage your partner to talk, listening carefully, commenting, praising or complimenting where appropriate (remember to focus actively on the things that you like, value and admire about your partner!).

What you're doing is setting the tone – keep it up without expecting anything in return. Be patient and you will be surprised how much you get back if you establish a positive, non-judgemental, non-critical, fun and accepting environment. Use the tips in the previous chapters about the things you can do to create a rewarding relationship.

EXAMPLE 4
Have you noticed that he stopped doing those little romantic gestures you used to love, like hiring a plane to write in large smoke letters 'I love you!' across the sky, or climbing that steep

hill just because you commented casually that you would love to have that pretty flower growing right at the top? Then maybe you should start paying attention to the other things he does to show that he loves you, like the occasional breakfast in bed, or making sure your car is MOT-ed and always clean and full of petrol. Of course you can do these things for yourself, but that's his way of showing that he cares.

Overcoming unrealistic expectations

When his untidiness is getting to you and you're tempted to be critical, remember that he really listens when you need him to. Remember the analogy of the coughing and the music. I could go on but I think you've probably got the idea by now.

Expectations can do more than sabotage a budding relationship or upset the honeymoon period. They can damage even apparently solid relationships. Here's an example as told to me by Jennifer: 'Philip was forty-eight when I first met him and I was thirty. He was so confident, successful, and running his own business. He was clearly well-off, but it wasn't his money that attracted me; he was so sophisticated and self-assured. He had obviously been around and used to take me to expensive restaurants, the opera and, occasionally, on trips abroad. He taught me a lot and I used to look up to him. We married six months after we met. Five years later he had a stroke. He's suddenly got so old and weak. We don't make love any more. Also, he made some bad financial decisions. I expected him to be strong and wise and now . . .' Her voice trailed off.

Her mistake was in expecting him always to be the strong one, not realising that in good marriages and partnerships people often have to take it in turns. Marrying people substantially older than you are is something to be undertaken only with very open eyes. Jennifer was unlucky or immature – take your pick. And poor Philip was very unlucky. Tragedies don't necessarily destroy relationships; but unrealistic expectations certainly do.

Let me give you another example. When Lynn and James married they were both in their mid-twenties. They never talked about having children. Lynn never really thought about it and just assumed that's what happens when people get married but, two years later, she realised that she didn't want to have children at all. James tried to persuade her, then pressure her. She resisted. They got divorced. If there is any blame to be handed out it's for making a seriously wrong assumption and never discussing their expectations of marriage and each other – before they got married. Because of that, when Lynn discovered how she really felt about having children, she changed the goal posts after the game had started – and that's nearly always a recipe for disaster.

Don't get discouraged! There is help!

What can I say to you to spare you the disappointments and heartache that unrealistic expectations can bring? Only you will know if your life is ruled by expectations, or whether you just have a few that you need to bring out into the open, dust off, examine and revise. But there are a couple of things you can do to help yourself:

1. Start by knowing yourself. Think about what's important to you, your values, needs, preferences, expectations and assumptions – and write them down. For additional 'inspiration', read Chapter 17, How to Recognise The Right Partner for You.
2. When you meet potentially promising people, find out what's important to them, how they see things, start asking the right questions, listen carefully to the answers, and observe how they act. For example, are their actions consistent with their words?

I hope you can now see how important it is for you to become aware of your own expectations, assumptions and needs – as well as those of the other person.

Another thing you can do, once you've become aware of your expectations, is to start questioning them. Ask yourself, for example:

- Is it true that men have to be confident and strong? Where is it written? Who says so? Does it mean that women shouldn't be strong and independent?
- Is it true that men have to change the plugs and women do the cooking? What about individual talents and preferences? What about individual choice?
- Is it true that it's the man's role to approach the woman? What if the woman is more outgoing and confident and happens to be attracted to a man who is a little shy? Does he really have to sit and wait and hope?

How can you tell if your expectations, assumptions and beliefs are so deep-rooted that they could sabotage your relationships? If your relationships (friendships and love) often go wrong and you tend to believe that it's always the other person's fault, then you may need more help than I can give you. There are many good therapists who can help you re-learn new and healthier expectations, beliefs and attitudes. However, I'm a little worried about the enormous numbers of counsellors and therapists around, some of whom sound more than a little dubious. So, if you think you need a little professional guidance try to ensure you put yourself in safe hands. There are two ways forward:

1. Go to your local doctor and ask him to refer you
2. Go privately

If you choose to go privately, you need to take extra care before you commit yourself. What I suggest you do is approach The Independent Psychology Service, Tel. 0181 883 9685 who have a list of reputable therapists. They will discuss with you very briefly what kind of help you need, and recommend how you should proceed. They also take into consideration where you live.

Reassessing your expectations and double-checking your assumptions is an important way to help you open yourself up to people as human beings as opposed to stereotypical figures. And, what's really wonderful, is that it frees you and your partner so you can become whole individuals, each with both so-called 'male' and 'female' qualities and talents, such as tenderness, independence, caring and confidence, or the ability to make sense of what happens under the hood of a car, cook a super meal, keep the finances in order and do the laundry – both of you! That means you can share the responsibilities according to your talents and preferences, and not according to whether you're a man or a woman.

TIPS

- Expectations can trip you up and endanger even the most promising relationships. Try to identify which are the ones that interfere with satisfying friendships and a fulfilling love relationship.
- Start to help yourself by clarifying your own expectations and finding out those of the other person.
- Question your expectations. Are they realistic? Are they true or false?
- If you need more help, ask your GP to refer you to a reputable psychotherapist or contact The Independent Psychology Service, Tel 0181 883 9685.

CHAPTER 9

Broken Love and New Beginnings

You may wonder why this chapter is in this book at all. I, too, wondered if it belonged here but I came to the conclusion that many of you may be in the process of ending a relationship, and wondering both if anybody will ever love you again and whether you will ever allow yourself to love again. To answer these questions, I truly believe you will. But what I want is for you to find a love that's really good for you. Whether you're newly single or have been single again for a while, you may still be feeling very bruised and vulnerable. You might not even understand what happened, why or how. You believed such things only happened to other people, not to you – you were so in love! I felt this chapter might help you understand what went wrong so you can take steps to prevent any new relationship following in the same way.

Grieving takes, needs and deserves time to enable you to heal. Use the time to reflect, to strengthen yourself, to get to know and like yourself again. Try to forgive yourself for any real or imaginary mistakes you may have made, but learn from them so you don't make them again. People often do when they rush into a new affair on the rebound.

In Chapter 7, Love: An Insider's Guide, I took a brief look at why love relationships break down. Those reasons were a start but they didn't tell the whole story; in this chapter I want to dig a little deeper.

I've come up with eleven reasons why relationships go

wrong; as I list them I indicate which chapter addresses that particular issue so you can find out how to side-step that danger:

1. Low self-esteem (read Chapter 24, How to Care for Yourself: The Magic of Self-Esteem)
2. Being too needy and expecting your partner to make you happy (I'm exploring this topic later on in this chapter)
3. Not communicating, which includes not listening (read Chapter 19, Listening – The Ultimate Aphrodisiac)
4. Past patterns. This is the hardest one on relationships because neither of you realises what's happening. You both carry 'old baggage' to the new relationship, usually in terms of resentments that you act out, again and again. You bring into the relationship two worlds of different perceptions and experiences, different needs and wants, and different expectations and memories so it's not surprising that you will also experience tensions, stresses, fears and anxieties, especially when you try to develop the intimacy you yearn for, yet feel too scared to open up to.

   If you find yourself repeating the same mistakes again and again, this could indicate that there's a pattern that is constantly tripping you up and sabotaging your efforts, in which case you will probably need more help than I can give you. If you need professional guidance, either go to your GP for referral or go privately. The Independent Psychology Service on 0181 883 9685 may be a good starting point.
5. Not having enough fun and rewarding time together (read Chapter 26, Laughter: The Missing Link)
6. Having unrealistic expectations and being judgemental (read the previous chapter, Expectations: They Can Make Your Relationship Fail!)
7. Being out of synch sexually and in terms of physical

affection (read Chapters 21 and 22, The Power of Touch and How to Develop a Fulfilling Sexual Relationship)
8. Having no plans, no direction and no common purpose. (Read Chapter 17, How to Recognise the Right Partner for You). Knowing what's important to you and getting to know the person with whom you want to spend the rest of your life includes finding out whether you share roughly similar goals. If you don't, you will end up growing apart.
9. Failure to show respect, appreciation and love. (Read Chapters 20 and 23, In Praise of Praise and How to Make Love)
10. Boredom! (Read Chapter 23, How to Make Love – but I have more to add on this subject later on in this chapter on pages 84 and 85).
11. Frequent unequal share of responsibility (read Chapter 23, How to Make Love).

The dangers of neediness

Being needy is a big issue in relationships and the first difficulty is that we often don't recognise ourselves as needy – it's our partner who complains about it. Usually, but by no means always, it's the woman who is needy and this neediness springs from feelings of low self-esteem, insecurity and doubts about her partner's love. One way this shows itself is wanting to spend all your free time together. This may also be one of your unrealistic expectations and be based on the hope that, by keeping him where you can see him, he won't go off and leave you. Well, I have news for you: it won't work. Men – people – tend to feel terribly stifled and the more you try to hang on to them the more they will want to get away.

How women can keep themselves interesting and their partners interested

Women, if you want to stay attractive to your partner, then I strongly suggest that you let him do his own thing. But more important than that, I suggest even more strongly that *you* do your own thing. This is the answer to keeping yourself interesting, with your self-esteem and your energy levels high. Do things that remind you of who you really are. Women often tend to lose themselves in relationships, pushing their dreams on to the back burner until the fire goes out. I've worked with women returners who want to go back to work but don't know what they want to do. They feel they have nothing to offer and they've even forgotten how to dream. The truth, of course, is not that they have nothing to offer but that they *believe* that they have nothing to offer – and it almost makes no difference which one it is. If you think you can't, then you can't – period.

Here are some tips to recharge your batteries, enhance your confidence and your sense of self:

- Spend time on your own, quietly, where you can sit and think, or just be. I know what you're thinking. You're thinking, 'Yes, I'd love that but where do I find the time?' How about locking the bathroom door and having a bubble bath with some scented moisturising gel and maybe some music – close your eyes, and drift away. Even half an hour will do wonders!

- Take an hour to enjoy reading a book. Don't give me any excuses about not having the time – if you *want* to do it (whatever 'it' may be), then you *will* find the time! (At work managers know that, if they want to get something done, they had better give the task to a busy person!)

- Go to an exhibition on your own, go to see a film, meet friends for a special meal and a chat, or a quick pizza and a Coke. It's not about spending lots of money, it's about doing things that remind you that you're an individual. All relationships have three identities: yours, your partner's and the relationship's. You are *not* your relationship. You are *you*. And don't you forget it.

- Look at the list you made of things that make your heart sing. It doesn't matter if it's short to start with. I promise

80

you will come up with more and more things that give you real joy and pleasure.

- Make your own decisions – don't always consult your partner about every little thing. If asked what you'd like to do, make a suggestion. Do *not* say, 'I don't mind. Whatever you want.' You're not being selfless and thoughtful; you're being foolish. A man won't be grateful, he'll get irritated. He'll think, 'Why can't she make up her mind for once?' or 'Why do I always have to decide?'

  I can hear you cry, 'But Jim loves me just as I am! He loves to look after me and make decisions!' Maybe, but I think you're fooling yourself. One day you *will* – not may – need to learn how to look after yourself, so you might as well start now. Otherwise you will never know how – and it can't get much scarier than that. Be your own best friend!

My friend Jonathan echoed the things men in my workshop look for in a woman, when he told me recently that he longs for a woman with whom he can share the decisions, the burdens and the joys. In fact, he's looking for an equal partner.

These are all ideas to keep you interested in yourself and in what's happening around you because if you're bored with yourself, other people will also be bored with you. On the other hand, if you're interested in what's going on, doing and learning and enjoying all sorts of things, then you can't help but become more interesting. Another virtuous circle! If you do something for yourself that turns you on, you will find, almost by accident, that your partner is also turned on.

How men can keep their partners truly in love with them

Now it's your turn, men. You too have to do something to keep your partner interested in you and what I suggest is exactly the opposite of my suggestion for women. You have to become less independent. Your partner needs to know that she's important to you, that you enjoy spending time with her, that you value

81

and respect her. And, if you've read this far, you'll know what you can do to make that happen.

So what can you do to make a woman feel loved? Here are some ideas to get you going but I would suggest, since we're all individuals, that you ask your partner as well.

- Say 'I love you'. Say it often and in as many different ways you can think of.
- Give her cuddles, massage her neck and shoulders, stroke her cheek, touch her hand. Physical affection breeds trust, tenderness and intimacy. For more ideas read Chapter 21, The Power of Touch.
- Be willing to share with her how you feel about things, your anxieties and fears, your moments of satisfaction and pleasure, your hopes and aspirations – both the little day-to-day things and the bigger things. One example of this might be how you feel about other people in your life such as your brother or sister, your mother or father, a colleague at work, your boss, how you are when you're with them, what works for you and what doesn't. These are very important issues because they shape your beliefs about people in general and make you the man you are.
- Tell her the truth. Don't pretend. For example, don't pretend to be confident when you feel shaky inside, don't pretend to be certain about something you're unsure about. Men often pretend because they believe their partner won't respect them if they knew they were not always strong and in control. Given the messages men have been fed most of their lives about how 'a real man' should be it is understandable that you feel anxious. But don't let that fear hold your feelings in. Ask yourself: 'Am I sure that my partner will be put off?' There are only three possible answers: 'Yes' – 'No' – 'I don't know.' And, since you can't look inside a person's heart, the true answer is, at best, 'I don't know.' So give yourself – and her – a chance to come closer together by

sharing your feelings. Your trust and your willingness to show the vulnerable part of you is a powerful way to make your partner feel loved.

- Make love to her – sometimes hotly and passionately, sometimes slowly and tenderly.
- Do notice the things she says and does that you admire, notice how she looks, express your appreciation, acknowledge her efforts, let her know how proud you are of her.
- Show an interest in what she does, what went well for her and what didn't – and listen to her without judging and without making her think she is wrong for feeling what she is feeling. It doesn't help to say things like, 'Don't worry' or 'Don't be silly'. And, most important of all, do it without trying to fix it for her. You will find that she is capable of sorting things out for herself; all she needs is to be truly heard. And that means that you can relax because all you have to do is to listen and to *be* there for her.
- Surprise her occasionally with a special treat, a meal cooked with your own fair hands, take her out to a nice restaurant, buy her flowers, tell her to put her feet up while you do the vacuuming (and do it!)
- Make time to be with her and let her know that your time alone together is precious to you.

Outside events that put a strain on your relationship

'Right,' I hear you – men and women – say, 'now I know what can put my relationship at risk.' Well, not quite. There's more. You don't exist in a vacuum. Things happen out there that can put you both under real strain – things over which you have little control . . . if any. Things such as:

- Bereavement
- Work changes, for example becoming successful, being made redundant, or going bankrupt

- Finances, for example making or winning a lot of money, or losing it
- Significant weight loss or weight gain (I will comment further on this in Chapter 12, Why Do Men . . .? Why Do Women . . .? Questions and Answers)
- Retirement, especially the unplanned and unwanted variety which is why it's so important to think about it in advance. If you're employed find out if your company runs pre-retirement programmes. Some companies also include the partner
- Health loss. A big one this
- Moving house. You lose contact with friends and your family, and move into a new neighbourhood where you don't know anybody. This is often linked to work relocation so the stresses are often compounded.

These triggers can bring a couple closer together, but sometimes they can drive them apart. That's especially so if they can't talk about it or, worse, if they start blaming each other. There's only one way out: you need to talk, listen, compromise, adapt and adjust. And you need to move towards one another, slowly and tentatively, however hurt you may feel, and learn to support each other again. I'm sure I don't have to spell out for you what the alternative is . . .

Is there more?

The things mentioned above are 'biggies' – but little things are often even more dangerous because they're so insidious. One or both of you may have let yourselves go – putting on weight, growing a beer belly, or becoming sloppy and just . . . well, unappealing – and then you wonder why your partner isn't sexually attracted to you any more. Take a good look in the mirror – and I mean a good look, without flinching. Now do something about it!

The other danger spot is boredom. In happy relationships,

the couple have found the right balance between stability and uncertainty. Some people, both men and women, fear this particular bogey and they sometimes rush off and try to deal with it in destructive ways, including having affairs. These people are particularly afraid of the word 'stability' because they believe that it's the same as 'boredom'. Others tend to distrust 'uncertainty'. Just to make things clear, by uncertainty I definitely don't mean not knowing what your partner is up to, wondering if you can count on them, who they're with, or even if they're going to come back at all. Nor do I mean by stability spending all your free time together, doing the same things over and over again, and getting into a boring rut. The secret is to find the balance between the *right kind* of stability and uncertainty. Only you and your partner can decide what your favourite 'ingredients' are and I've already given you lots of ideas but here are a few more, just to give you a kick-start:

You might like to start the week by arranging a surprise treat for your partner (it can be anything from a bunch of flowers, a box of their favourite chocolates, a bottle of wine or whatever you know would please them). One evening you might do something on your own, go to the gym, go to the pub with your mates, play squash or golf, have a meal with friends, visit your parents on your own, stay in and read a book, listen to music or watch your favourite TV programme. Another day you might like to go out together. The idea is to look forward to being together again. This is how anticipation works: looking forward to something makes us appreciate it more.

People often complain, not surprisingly, that they're totally exhausted after work. They think that flopping down in front of the telly after dinner is restful. They're wrong! It just makes you more lethargic.

I remember one day when I was a child I'd just finished doing my homework and I was feeling bored and listless. My dad told me to help Mum with the dishes. Boring! I grumbled that I was tired. Then Dad added the magic words: 'Afterwards we'll go to the cinema.' Well! I never perked up so fast before! It sounded like *fun*! Dad laughed and said 'See? You're not so tired any more. Go and help Mum with the dishes.' Yes, of course I felt deflated but the point had been made. And it's just the same here. Some activity that you really enjoy, something you can look forward to is extremely invigorating as well as fun. And it's also an insurance against either one of you looking for fun outside the home – with someone else.

How to Keep Your Relationship Alive

Let's finish then on a positive note. This is a good place to summarise the key learning points, as we say in the trade:

- Love yourself as you really are, unconditionally, no ifs or buts.
- Learn to love others just as unconditionally. If you've managed the previous one, then this one will be a piece of cake.
- Teach each other how to touch, both sexually and non-sexually.
- Be open. Don't pretend to feel OK when you're not feeling OK. Don't be defensive. It doesn't help nor does it get you what you want. Ask yourself, why are you feeling attacked? Try to talk about it without blaming, judging or accusing. I didn't say this would be easy, only that you do have to do it.
- Keep the communication channels open. Keep sharing your thoughts and feelings, your hopes and dreams, your fears and anxieties, your successes and disappointments. People often think that there are only two options: dependence or independence. But there is a third one: inter-dependence. That's what you need to aim for, otherwise you'll wake up one morning beside a total stranger.
- Listen to each other. This is especially hard when you're feeling hurt but, if you've been listening all along, then it won't be as hard as if you haven't.

- Find opportunities for shared laughter, shared humour, shared fun, and shared good times together.
- Be compassionate and tolerant and be sure you're absolutely clear – long before you even enter a relationship – what's important to you, what you can live with and what is completely unacceptable to you. Then stop nagging! Treat each other with at least the same politeness you reserve for strangers.
- Do not, under any circumstances, try to change your partner. Acceptance is the key that encourages and supports change – if they want to change.
- Give them lots of acknowledgement, praise, support and encouragement. See the love behaviours of happily married couples in Chapter 7, Love: An Insider's guide.
- Make yourself happy – don't wait for your partner or anybody else to do it for you. (Read Chapter 25, The Art of Being Happy).
- Take account of the differences between men and women in terms of how they talk, how they think and feel and react, in the way they handle stress, their sexual needs and how they want to be loved (read Chapter 15, Men and Women: Are We Really So Different from Each Other?). Remember, they're not bloody-minded and they're not doing it – whatever 'it' may be – just to annoy you. At least not unless they really are annoyed and want to get back at you.
- Discuss your expectations well in advance and try (and I mean try – after all, there are no guarantees) not to change the goal posts once you're in a relationship.

TIPS

- If you're ending or have just ended a relationship, give yourself time to grieve and time to heal.
- With the help of this chapter, reflect on what went wrong and how you may have contributed to the break-up. Learn from your mistakes.

- Women, don't force your partner – and don't let him force you – into spending all your free time together.
- Women, maintain or develop your own identity. Do things that interest you and you will remain or become more interesting, both to yourself and to others.
- Men, the strong, silent type has gone out of fashion. Show your partner that she's important to you, that you enjoy her company, and that you like, value and respect her.
- Women, men also need to know that.
- Events outside your control may put heavy stress on your relationship. You need to combat this by keeping friendly and loving communication channels open.
- Men and women, don't let yourselves go.
- Men and women, find the right balance between stability and uncertainty.
- Men and women, familiarise yourselves with the learning points in this chapter.

CHAPTER 10

What Attracts People to One Another?

There is a lot of speculation about what attracts people to one another, especially that magical initial attraction that draws people together like a magnet. Less thought tends to be given, however, to how attraction works to *keep* people together.

Initial Attraction

What is it that attracts people to one another? (In this context I'm using the word 'attract' in a general way, to include both attracting potential friends as well as potential lovers. Attraction is the key to getting any kind of relationship off the ground, and that applies not only to love and friendships but to business relationships as well, though in that case people tend to use another word – rapport – which is basically the same thing.) When we first meet somebody new, what attracts us are a number of things, a 'package', of which physical appearance is only one part. Obviously, we all have certain general preferences but, time and time again in my workshops both men and women have commented that often the person they ended up falling in love with looked nothing like their fantasy.

Research into how people decide if they want to get to know somebody has shown that people make judgements based on three elements, and that what makes these elements so powerful is that they operate not only on a conscious level but, more importantly, on a subconscious level as well. And it is crucial that we understand this for two reasons:

A. This is something you can't fight, so it's useless to complain how unfair life is.
B. There's a lot you can do to influence how people see you.

The three elements that have such an influence are:

1. How you look
2. How you sound
3. What you say.

That's fine as far as it goes, but there are a few surprises. Let's assume that all these three elements together make up 100 per cent.

1. The biggest impact of the lot is made by how you *look*. This accounts for 55 per cent. More about this in a moment because there's more to it than meets the eye.
2. Next comes how you *sound* and that makes up another 38 per cent of the total impression.
3. Finally, a poor third, with a tiny 7 per cent of the overall impact, comes what you actually *say*!

I have devoted a whole chapter to the third point, Chapter 15, 'Do You Come Here Often?' and Other Openings to Avoid, so let's look at the first two of these elements in more detail, starting with the rather controversial visual element.

Part of the visual attraction – though a less significant one than many of us believe – has to do with looks, and that includes, not surprisingly, height, build, shape, colouring, and so on. All this is a matter of personal taste but, as I found from the workshops, it isn't necessarily cast in stone.

Two additional things contribute to the impact:

a) Our choice of clothes
b) Our body language.

a) *Clothes*

We don't often stop to think about what our clothes say about us, so let's begin with the obvious and move on to the less obvious messages, starting with grooming. Grooming tells the world what we think about ourselves, our sense of self-esteem and self-respect. Let me give you two examples, both fairly extreme to make the point:

EXAMPLE 1

The first sign that somebody is becoming depressed because of, say, bereavement or redundancy, is that they let themselves go. They neglect themselves and their appearance, and stop caring.

EXAMPLE 2

Spending ages and ages in front of the mirror, trying to look like a model – unless, of course, that's how you earn your living – could indicate that you are a little bit too involved with yourself, perhaps at the expense of other things or other people.

Still under clothes comes our personal style. You may find this a little hard to believe, but it's through our choice of style that we express our taste, our personality, our values, and our attitude to life. Just stop for a minute and look at the people around you in the street. See that man? He's clean-shaven, is wearing a business suit, and carrying a briefcase. What kind of person do you imagine him to be? And that young man over there. He's wearing jeans, army surplus jacket, sneakers, and carries a rucksack. Which of the two do you believe is more likely to be a free spirit? Which is more likely to drive a car and have a mortgage? Which of the two is more likely to go camping and which might prefer to stay at a nice hotel? I'm not asking you to work out the truth, only to make an assumption based on your gut feeling.

And, if you are a woman dressed in jeans, T-shirt and perhaps you have a butterfly tattooed on your shoulder, which of the two men do you think is more likely to try and catch your eye? If you plumped for the young man in jeans, you win. And the reason is that you two are more likely to be kindred souls. All this happens quite subconsciously and is just one of the ways we pigeonhole and stereotype one another. How can you use this information to make it work for you?

First, think about the kind of people you'd like to attract. Then look at the way you dress, to see if this is likely to help or hinder you.

By the way, of course I believe you when you tell me about how your Aunt Sally went to the bakers around the corner, looking like death warmed up and nursing a horrible cold, and met this gorgeous man, who just happened to be buying his bagels there and how they're now happily married.

This book is about general principles, not individual cases, and the point of all this information is that, if you're not satisfied with the kind of people you're currently attracting, then perhaps your choice of clothes may – and I repeat, may – have something to do with it. And, by the way, no style is also a style: it's the 'I-couldn't-care-less' style.

One last word about physical attractiveness. It might interest you to know that this is just as important in friendships as it is in romance. That's because we prefer the company of people who are similar to us, people who are neither a lot more nor a lot less attractive than ourselves; otherwise we would not feel too comfortable in their company. Unfair? Maybe, but still true!

b) Body language

Let's now turn to something else that most dramatically affects people's perception of our attractiveness: our body language. It is through our body language that we communicate things like whether we're friendly or distant, lively or serious, confident or shy, happy or sad, tense or relaxed, angry or laid back – and all without saying a word. Of the three ingredients of the visual element – appearance, clothes and body language – it is our body language that is the most powerful and which has such a profound impact on the way people see us.

First watch your posture. Do you tend to stand erect or do you tend to slouch? Posture conveys a lot of information, such as whether you're bored, miserable, uninterested or tired, or whether you're full of energy and having a good time. If you want to project an image that is confident, friendly and approachable, start by keeping an open posture, that is any posture that feels comfortable to you except folding your arms across your chest because people tend to interpret this as a 'keep out' message.

Look out for any nervous habits you may have like biting your lower lip, playing with your hair, biting your nails, mooching around or shuffling which make you appear passive and unsure of yourself.

The next tip is particularly important: Do get into the habit of looking people in the eye. When people appear to avoid looking at us, we tend to suspect them of being untrustworthy or 'shifty', or even of not liking us and whether or not this is true is, unfortunately, completely irrelevant. If you catch somebody's eye and smile, that's usually interpreted as a sign that you're confident, friendly and that you enjoy meeting new people. And people who come across as friendly and approachable are also more likely to be seen as attractive. So do give it a try!

Now your facial expression. Sometimes we go around deep in thought without realising that we're scowling or frowning until some wise-guy – usually a complete stranger – comes up to us and says, 'Cheer up! It may never happen!' Yes, it is a bit of a cheek but it's useful to know if we come across as bad-tempered – even if we aren't. If people have commented on this before, try to develop a friendly expression instead when you feel yourself frowning. Practise different expressions in front of the mirror. You may think this sounds a little strange, but it is a very useful way to develop a new habit in the privacy of your own home, because the mirror gives you instant information about how others see you.

If you're not sure how you come across to people, ask someone you trust to give you honest feedback in terms of your body language and whether you have any irritating mannerisms or nervous habits.

c) How you sound

Let's turn now to the third element which is how you sound. Voice is something that women tend to notice more than men and, as you will see from Chapter 11, Men and Women: What Do We Want from Each Other?, women are attracted to a pleasant voice. What is a pleasant voice? This is a personal matter but what makes a voice appealing or irritating is how it sounds, for example whether it's deep or squeaky or light. (In the business world, women with light, 'little-girl' voices can have difficulty establishing their credibility and authority.) Sometimes we can really fall for an appealing tone of voice. There are some voices which are wonderfully sexy and you could sit listening to them all night . . . If you're not happy with how your voice sounds, then going to a voice coach could be the answer for you.

The way you sound also depends on things such as whether you speak loudly or softly; too fast or too slow; what accent you have; whether you keep interrupting or whether you allow long pauses before you respond; whether your voice is monotonous or lively; and whether you speak sharply (which could be interpreted as being aggressive).

Can you see now how much of an impact you can make before you have thought of something to say – witty or not?

Lasting Attraction

Let's now look at the other kind of attraction, the one that ensures that a couple stays together. The signs of the first kind of attraction, the gazing into each other's eyes, holding hands and being totally absorbed in each other are not in the least bit frivolous. In fact, they're extremely important because it is the initial attraction that brings a couple together and bonds them.

Couples who have been together for some time may stop doing the gazing, hand-holding, and so on, so what is it that continues to keep them together? It really is terribly straightforward. Initial attraction has changed into lasting attraction, which grows when the couple continues to like each other. Simple, isn't it? But not necessarily easy.

As time goes on, romance becomes less important while being able to live together in harmony becomes much more so. Here we are then, back to rewards. To use accountancy as an analogy, if you have more good times together than bad, then you're likely to continue being attracted to each other. If, however, you are 'in the red', then your relationship may go bankrupt.

What do I mean by liking? Liking comes out of sharing similar attitudes, values, likes and dislikes, goals, dreams and aspirations. The difference is that, while in the beginning what might have brought you together was your mutual enjoyment of, say, sports, dancing, Humphrey Bogart films, spaghetti or a similar taste in authors, you now need to be similar in other ways too, for example, attitudes towards both your careers, having versus not having children and how to bring them up, attitudes towards spending money versus saving it, who pays for what, issues about decision-making and consultation, how to spend your free time, and so on. It will help you here to go through Chapter 17, How to Recognise the Right Partner for You.

What often makes relationships go wrong is that, though people spend a lot of time getting to know each other, they often don't get to know each other well enough. There are reasons for this which, while understandable at the time, do not justify the enormous risk to the future happiness of your life and your relationship. What happens is that once we have found that wonderful person, the one we've always been looking for – he's so kind, she's so considerate, he's so thoughtful, she's such fun to be with – we don't want to do anything that might spoil things. Let me give you a few examples:

EXAMPLE 1
Still in the early days, you go out for dinner and you notice that your companion is drinking a lot and becomes a bit louder than usual. You've noticed this once or twice before but, instead of saying to yourself, 'Oh – oh! Watch out!', you say to yourself, 'Well, he's been working so hard lately, poor soul, he does need to unwind.'

EXAMPLE 2
While you are with friends, she makes some sarcastic remarks about you and everybody laughs. You feel hurt but, instead of nipping that right in the bud the minute you're alone together, you say to yourself, 'Well, she was only joking. She didn't really mean it.'

EXAMPLE 3
You're still in the process of getting to know each other and, during one of your conversations, he tells you things that indicate that he thinks that women are not to be trusted and that they're all after a fat wallet. This is one clue you can't afford to ignore. I know you can't imagine it now but, believe me, this is how he will treat you after the initial glow has dimmed – with suspicion, jealousy and possibly even with contempt.

EXAMPLE 4
You're having dinner at a nice restaurant and he makes a point of sending the wine back, complains loudly about the food and is rude to the waiter. Here's another vital clue about how you will end up being treated.

And so it goes, with all those little warning voices being forcibly shut up. Let me assure you that you ignore them at your peril. Why things so often go wrong is because important questions that should be asked, aren't, and warning signals that should be heeded, are ignored. Obviously no one is perfect, but what I'm talking about here are fundamentals on which you must not compromise.

Let me add one other bit of information. There have been studies which looked particularly at wives (because it's more often women who tend to initiate separation and divorce proceedings) and how happy they were compared with how long they had been dating before getting married. What they found was that, those who had got married after only knowing their partner less than five months were the least happy while those who had gone out together more than two years were happiest. The conclusion is clear: the longer you spend building the relationship and, in particular, the friendship, the more time you spend really getting to know each other, the more likely you are to increase your chances of happiness. Whatever you do, make sure you enter what will be the most important relationship of your life with your eyes wide open.

TIPS

- Think about the kind of people you want to attract. Then take a good look at your choice of clothes. Does it help or hinder you?
- As far as your body language is concerned, ask someone you trust to tell you honestly how you come across. Ask them to comment on your posture, your mannerisms, your facial expression, the way you speak – and ask them for tips on how to improve. Now ask one or two others, just to be sure.
- Be sure you make friends with potential romantic partners. This will help you form a more solid and lasting relationship.

- Make sure you share fundamental attitudes, values, likes and dislikes, goals, dreams and aspirations. Read Chapter 17, How to Recognise the Right Partner for You.
- Really get to know the person you want to spend the rest of your life with. Don't be reluctant to ask uncomfortable questions or to heed uncomfortable clues to their personality.

CHAPTER 11

Men and Women: What Do We Want from Each Other?

The sexual revolution and the women's movement have led to many very important changes, for example, in the way we perceive one another. We no longer regard woman as the 'Jane' to man's 'Tarzan'. At least that's what our brain tells us. Unfortunately, our gut feelings often let us down in the assumptions we make about one another. This shouldn't really surprise us when we consider how much we are bombarded and influenced by television ads, women's and men's magazines, romantic novels, and films, as well as the way we were brought up. On top of all that, our same-sex friends are likely to have similar ideas to ours and so keep supporting and strengthening them, without ever really questioning whether or not they are true.

The problem is that, if we expect people to be like our fantasies and stereotypes, we may be in for a bumpy ride, especially if, instead of seeing a man or a woman as an individual, we see them as typical of their sex – whatever 'typical' may mean. This set of ideas about how men and women are supposed to behave has created a lot of confusion about what we want in a partner so that we end up wanting conflicting things.

Here is an example: Suzanne is always complaining that George is closed and distant. 'He never talks to me,' she says,

'We just don't communicate any more, and we've only been together a little under a year.' She feels he's trying to keep her at arm's length. George sees things very differently. 'She's always complaining that I don't talk about my feelings, but she only really wants to talk about us and how I feel about her or something lovie-dovie. I know she needs reassuring, but so do I! When I start talking about how I worry that I might be made redundant, or the problem with keeping up with all those bills, or when I get really involved with cricket and want to explain the rules to her, she doesn't want to know. Apparently it's only OK to talk about some things, and some feelings, but not others. I wish she would make up her mind. Does she want me to be open or doesn't she?'

The problem often is that, on the one hand, a woman wants a man to be sensitive and, on the other, in control, someone who is vulnerable but also strong, gentle and ambitious, a man who can share his feelings, but who can also make her feel safe. With all those mixed messages no wonder men end up confused.

Men have come to realise that they can't always be the proverbial steady rock. Their dilemma is that they are not sure how far they can show it, how far they can trust their partner to accept them as they are, warts and all. If they're not sure, they are likely to clam up and not take the risk.

Men also have conflicting views and expectations of women. For example, a man will say he likes smart, independent and successful women but only as long as she is prepared to rearrange her life around his. So women feel somewhat confused too. We need to learn to understand and accept each other as we really are, individuals in our own right. Otherwise we will end up feeling hurt, resentful and misunderstood.

One of the sessions in my workshop, Men and Women: What Do we Want from Each Other?, makes a start by bringing these sometimes conflicting views out into the open. It also gives men and women the opportunity to think these questions through for themselves, to listen to each other, and even to challenge each other's views and opinions. The exercise starts with the men and the women discussing among themselves, openly and frankly, what they look for in a member of the opposite sex. I'm going to give you the results of this exercise because it adds the views of 'real' men and women to the findings of social research. They coincide, so I'm able to set out a rounded picture of what people look for in a potential partner.

Women
The things women look for in a man fall under six headings:

1. *Affection and kindness* Someone who is willing and able to listen, to express an interest in them, to behave in a kind and considerate way, who is able to show physical affection and warmth, is supportive, loyal, courteous, and generous with his time and money,
2. *Things in common* Someone who shares the same interests and values, is easy to talk with and has generally similar attitudes,
3. *Self-confidence* A man who likes strong, independent and clever women, who accepts gracefully when a woman occasionally pays her share. He has a sense of humour, doesn't take himself too seriously, a man who allows himself to be sometimes strong and sometimes vulnerable, who is reliable and trustworthy, and keeps his promises, however small.
4. *Honesty* He doesn't play games!
5. *Success* A man who is financially secure or who at least has a job when they first meet, who knows where he wants to go in life.
6. *Physical attractiveness* For women, this seems to mean mostly 'sexy' eyes, eyes that 'have a twinkle, a sparkle, that show warmth, and kindness', and even eyes that 'have a smile'. Those are the kind of eyes that make women go weak

at the knees. After that come 'a pleasant voice' and 'nice hands'. So far, women have not mentioned 'tight buttocks' which, according to some magazine articles, women are supposed to like, but this may still come.

Women particularly dislike men who are arrogant and patronising, self-absorbed, who drink and smoke to excess (non-smokers are being increasingly preferred), who make assumptions about women on the basis of a stereotype, who look for a 'mother', or who are either too intense or too emotionally distant.

Men
The things men look for in a woman fall under four headings:

1. *Physical appearance*   Although this tends to come top of the list, what men consider attractive varies a lot, contrary to what many women seem to believe. It includes women who are curvy or have a boyish figure, who are blonde or dark, tall or petite, who have hair that is short or long, straight or curly; so everyone will be attractive to some man.

   Anyway all that seems to be less important than that a woman should generally look after herself, have good dress sense (which, translated, means what this particular man likes), and be approachable, friendly and responsive. Age did not seem to be particularly important as long as it was not much more than five years either side of the man's.

   On the subject of beauty and physical attraction I have found two quotations which generally reflect the comments made by the men:
   - One is by Picasso who said: 'Academic training in beauty is a sham. When we love a woman, we do not start measuring her legs.'
   - The other is by Voltaire who said: 'Beauty, madam, pleases the eyes only; sweetness of disposition charms the soul.'

2. *Warmth* This means being warm-hearted and happy. As the men put it, they want a woman 'who makes me feel at ease', 'who appreciates my efforts', 'who shows warmth and compassion for my weaknesses', 'who has a sense of humour' and 'who doesn't take herself too seriously'.
3. *Social skills* This means being well-informed and able to talk about a wide range of topics, being interesting, relaxed and fun to be with. It also means a woman who is a good listener.
4. *Confidence and ambition* By this, men refer to a woman who is independent, who likes herself, is confident, has a good job but *'doesn't allow it to take her over'* (my italics: conflicting expectations rear their ugly head yet again), and who has a life and interests of her own. There were also some men, and not just the older ones, who were looking for a woman who would look after the home, irrespective of whether or not she had a full-time job (well, no surprises there!).

Men indicated that they especially dislike women who are judgemental, critical and aggressive and who try to control or manipulate them; also clingy or needy women and, particularly, women who try to 'improve' them.

Not surprisingly, this session is extremely lively, but what is striking about the final lists is how similar they are. The words used by the men and the women may be different, but the sentiments are certainly the same. For example, the women say that they want a man 'who listens to me', 'who shows an interest in me', and 'who is physically affectionate', while the men say they want a woman 'who appreciates my efforts', 'shows warmth and compassion for my weaknesses', 'is not critical or judgemental' and 'doesn't nag'. All this can be translated into 'makes me feel special'. Wanting to be treated in a kind, warm and supportive way is the thread that runs through both lists.

When we examine some of these statements in more detail, the discussions become really animated. For example, as women expect, one of the first things on every man's list is a woman who is physically attractive, though that does not mean that every man is looking for a woman who is tall, slim, who has long, blonde hair and legs that go all the way up to her neck. In fact, once they start explaining what they meant by 'attractive', individual men give strikingly different descriptions, and they qualify this by adding that appearance is only important when they first meet the woman. Afterwards it's their personality that wins – or loses – the day.

Some women dislike being judged according to their physical appearance, forgetting that they, too, rate a man's looks important enough to include on their list, even though usually near the bottom. Another difference between men and women is that, when it comes to appearance, they tend to look at different parts of the body. Men often look at body shape, although lately they seem to mention eyes and a warm smile more and more often. Women, on the other hand, place the eyes at the top of the list. The only area in which both men and women agreed, as far as physical attractiveness is concerned, is grooming. Both like people who take pride in their appearance without being vain.

Only men mention age when listing their requirements, and of those only very few in the older age group specifically mention that they prefer young women.

The last few chapters as well as this one have painted a picture of the kind of qualities people regard as important and how they can enable you to build lasting friendships and love relationships. This is useful to help you identify which ones you may need to develop and which you may need to improve if you want a fulfilling social and personal life. No one can be forced to change but, should you feel that learning new skills and discovering new ideas and insights will get you what you want, then this is the book for you.

I would, however, like to make two important points:

1. Don't ever pretend to be something you are not. For example, as a woman, you might want to hide the fact that you are strong, capable, independent with your own views and opinions, because you think that men prefer women who are agreeable, easy-going, who always defer to their judgement, choices and decisions. As a matter of fact, most men I have spoken with don't really like this kind of woman; they prefer women on whom they can count to be a partner and a friend.

If you are a man you might be tempted to pretend that you are better off than you really are, or that you have a more interesting job than you actually have because you think that women are attracted by wealth and power.

There is no doubt that just being ourselves can sometimes feel scary, especially if we're afraid that we might not be good enough. However, picture the following scenario. Imagine you meet someone you really fancy and that, in order to get them interested in you, you present whatever 'desirable' image you think will work with that person. Now imagine that it worked. That person is really hooked on you — in fact, they think you're their dream come true! Wouldn't that be wonderful?

Well, actually no, it wouldn't. I will go even further and say that it would be a real tragedy, because it could ruin two people's lives — yours, because how long can you keep up the pretence without cracking under the strain of it all? How long before you end up resenting your partner for not loving you as you really are, when the truth is that you tricked them in the first place? And you could also ruin your partner's, because you will have manipulated them into believing you are someone else. Now you're both trapped, and all because you didn't trust yourself to be as you really are. Not a happy outcome, is it?

By being ourselves, we stand a better chance of meeting the person who will be the right one for us, either as a friend or as a lover, someone who accepts us and loves us as we really are, warts and all.

2. There is always room for improvement and, when I suggest you might like to develop new qualities and skills and work on some of your shortcomings, I mean things such as the following: taking people for granted, interrupting, not listening, nagging, criticising and having unrealistic expectations.

You might also find it helpful to look back over previous relationships, to see what you can learn from them. What part did you play in the breakdown? Did you expect your partner to fill the empty gaps in your life instead of filling them for yourself? Did you ever put yourself in your partner's – or friend's – shoes and were you able to listen to them without becoming defensive? Think back: is there a common pattern to your past break-ups?

Another useful thing to do is polish your 'people skills', those that make it easier for us to get along with one another. Experiment with different ways of doing things. Taking the initiative, and taking control of our lives, makes us stronger because we will begin to like ourselves a whole lot better and our self-esteem and confidence will grow when we start seeing results. That's what I call a 'virtuous' or positive circle.

TIPS
- Think about what you're looking for in a potential partner taking account of your own needs, values and preferences. See Chapter 17, How to Recognise the Right Partner for You.
- Don't pretend to be anything other than who you are. That's a sure-fire recipe for attracting the wrong people.
- Identify any bad habits you may have that tend to alienate people.
- Identify the qualities and skills that you need to acquire or work on in order to improve your chances of developing a fulfilling social and personal life.

- Learn from past mistakes. Reflect about how you might have contributed to the breakdown of your past relationships.
- Try out new things and work on different ways of operating. Pay attention to how you're progressing and make adjustments where necessary. But don't change your approach too soon. Be patient and give things a chance to work.

CHAPTER 12

Why Do Men . . .?
Why Do Women . . .?
Questions and Answers

In all my workshops there is a session when men and women can ask each other all sorts of questions. This is a unique opportunity to find out what makes others tick and to ask the kinds of questions you wouldn't ask on a one-to-one basis. The issues raised are generally very broad yet the same kinds of questions tend to come up again and again in other workshops. For the sake of clarity, I will use a question and answer format and add further information where appropriate.

Q: *Why do men say they'll phone you and then don't?*
This is top of the list and gets asked at almost every workshop. This is what the men have to say:

A: • 'I'm not sure how to say: "I enjoyed the evening but don't particularly want to repeat it".'
 • 'I think it's expected of me.'
 • 'I don't know how else to round off the evening.'

Since this particular issue is a real bugbear for women, let's see if we can shed a little light on what is happening. The phone is probably the biggest hurdle men and women have to surmount to establish a relationship because, unless the call is made, nothing can happen.

Women tend to be especially prone to sitting by the phone, staring at it, willing it to ring and cursing it when it doesn't. Then they start to agonise about where they've gone wrong, they wish they'd said 'X' or that they hadn't said 'Y'. In short, they take it terribly personally. Alternatively, they get angry at themselves for even minding.

Many women still believe that, if the man is interested, he will ask her for her phone number and that the extent of her choice is whether or not to give it to him. Then, all she can do is wait. Of course, that's no longer true. You can still give him your phone number if you want to but you can also ask him for his, and you don't have to wait for him to ring, like a good little girl. You can take the initiative and ring him. When you do, keep it light and say something along the lines of, 'A friend gave me two tickets to . . . Would you like to come?' or 'I'm having a party and I'm asking a few friends round; would you like to come along?'

From the men's comments, you can see they feel that asking a woman for her phone number is the only polite way to end an evening, and probably even believe that it would be rude not to ask. A man may not even be sure at that stage whether or not he would like to see the woman again. He hasn't thought that far ahead, there may be other things on his mind which have nothing to do with her, or he might only have wanted a pleasant evening, not a relationship.

Sometimes it may simply be a question of timing. One of the rewarding things about my work, is that people love to tell me their stories. Here is one of them, the story of Simon. He met Gina at a party. They spent the whole evening together and, in his own words, had a great time. Then, once the evening was over, that was that. About a year later and quite by accident, they met at another party. Once again, they spent the whole evening together and once again had a great time. Only on this occasion Simon thought he would like to see Gina again. And now they're going out together and he thinks she's the best thing since sliced bread!

I asked him why he hadn't invited her out that first time. His answer? It was nothing she said or didn't say. The thought hadn't even crossed his mind – maybe it just wasn't the right time. Who knows?

I love this story because I finally got the answer to a question that had been plaguing me for so long. Like just about every other woman I know, I used to think that if two people have a nice time together, surely they would both want to do it again. Apparently, that's too easy. The real answer is 'not necessarily' and it's not something the man works out consciously. For many men, once the evening is over, that's that.

Sometimes conversations or dates, even very enjoyable ones, are a very pleasant way of passing the time and nothing more, while, other times, they may be the beginning of a friendship that may or may not turn to love. The important thing is to enjoy the present, enjoy the conversation or the date for what they are, a nice way to spend the time with someone. Don't expect it necessarily to turn into anything else; if it does, that's a bonus. Meanwhile, go out and carry on meeting other people.

So, all you women out there, please, lighten up on this! Don't plan your future around one date. Enjoy it while it lasts, but don't spend the next week waiting for the phone to ring. Remember that asking for your phone number is part of the dating ritual and that there's no guarantee that he will phone you.

Q: *How do men feel about being asked out by a woman?*

A: So far, without exception, the men say that they would like it very much but add that this has rarely, if ever, happened to them. The reason they would welcome it, they say, is because it would take the pressure off them always having to be the ones to put themselves on the line.

Women, on the other hand, have ambivalent feelings about asking men out, and fall into three categories:

1. Some do call men and ask them out while facing up to the fact that, as men have always known, sometimes it works and sometimes it doesn't.
2. Others admit that they don't like to ask men out for fear of rejection. To these women I say that, as my workshop makes clear, men prefer women who are confident rather than passive, and waiting is passive. Confidence is sexy, so go for it, even if you feel wobbly inside! Some men will be delighted to hear from you and others won't. Accept that you couldn't possibly be everybody's cup of tea – why should you be? Haven't you ever met people you didn't particularly warm to? Or people you enjoyed talking with without wanting to meet them again? I rest my case.
3. And finally, there is a very small minority of women who firmly believe that it's up to the man to do the asking, which to me seems a great shame because it closes them off from lots of potentially fulfilling friendships.

Q: *How soon do men want sex after meeting a woman?*

A: Replies varied. Some said, only half tongue-in-cheek, that if they fancied the woman, as quickly as possible; while others enjoyed the 'getting-to-know-each-other' period.

Q: *What do men think of women who have sex on the first date?*

A: All the men responded; if it feels right for both of you, do it.

However we all know that it's not as simple as that. The man is expected to be the hunter while the woman is expected to set the pace. Whatever the man says, there may be a sneaky suspicion in his head – afterwards, of course – that she should have put the brakes on. He may even wonder, since she had sex with him on the first date, if she might not be a little too free with her body. I'm not convinced that the issue is a moral one; rather I suspect it's to do with the man wanting to feel special rather than one of many.

One important difference between men and women when it comes to sex is that, generally, men feel that sex is one thing and a relationship quite another, while women seem to need to be in love before they can truly enjoy sex. Many men push really hard for sex and the woman often allows herself to be talked into it, even if she isn't quite ready. (It is also not unknown for the woman to seduce the man before he is ready. Contrary to popular myth, men are not sex machines.) This explains why there is so much potential for confusion, misunderstandings and hurt.

There are a number of angles to this dilemma. Women, you have to face the fact, however hard you may find to accept it, that men don't need to be *in* love in order to *make* love.

Men, you have a brain and you don't need to manipulate a woman to get her into bed.

Both of you need to think about why you want to make love and discuss it honestly and tactfully. If either of you feels that the other is moving too fast and you're not ready to make love just yet, then say so without destroying the other person's ego or making them feel rejected. This is discussed in more detail in Chapter 21, How to Develop a Fulfilling Sexual Relationship.

Q: *Can men have platonic relationships?*

A: Yes, provided the man doesn't fancy the woman.

Q: *Who is supposed to pay?*
This issue is a 'biggie' and one that still makes both men and women feel a little uncomfortable.

A small minority of women argue that the man should always pay, on the grounds that he usually earns more than the woman; some say that if they don't they're 'cheap'. And there have even been one or two women who have claimed that the man should pay because, 'after all they're enjoying the pleasure of my company'. I only include this comment because, to my mind, it's such an outrageous one. Thank goodness these views are vastly outnumbered by those of the majority of sensible and sensitive women. This is, however, another example of how rigid expectations can hamper a developing friendship.

Men say that they don't mind paying as long as it isn't always them and women say they would like to pay sometimes, but are not sure how to broach the subject in case they offend the man.

A: The right answer is, 'It depends on the situation'. Generally, the person who does the asking does the paying (or, at the very least, offers to pay, especially the first time). At the same time, you both need to be absolutely clear that the mere fact that one person has paid gives them no rights whatsoever over the other person. You may be as surprised as I was to find it even necessary to mention this in this day and age.

Having said that, an easy-going and relaxed way of handling the matter, especially for women, is to say with a smile before ordering, 'Today is my treat, your turn is next time.' It should be done in a totally matter-of-fact way, without making a big deal out of it – which, of course, it isn't. It also makes you come across as confident and works particularly well after you have been out a couple of times and the man has always paid until then.

Going Dutch is OK but, if you do it too often, you may be seen as a bit too controlling. It can also keep people distant from each other, because treating someone is a friendly gesture, as is letting someone else treat you.

114

Q: *Why do men change the minute they're sure of the woman?*

A: It's all part of the chase. The hunt is over and they can go back to real life. Some men even regard women who don't understand that as clingy.

Although this question is asked mostly by women, both men and woman change. When this happens the partner gets upset, though different things bother men and women. Women get upset by the fact that the man is no longer as attentive and romantic as he used to be when they were dating. The real issue for women, I suspect, is that they feel taken for granted and invisible – an issue I feel passionate about.

It's not only men who change, though, women do too. Men are bothered when their partner changes in appearance, like putting on a lot of weight, though even dramatic weight loss can be very unsettling too. Or they are upset when their partner changes for example, by becoming more independent and ambitious. The issue for men is that they hate change of any kind and when it comes about they feel cheated and threatened.

The problem with losing weight is that the man is likely to feel threatened by suddenly having a more attractive partner than he originally bargained for. He may fear that men are going to start coming on to her, and that she'll go off him, start having affairs, or even leave him altogether. I'm not saying don't lose weight; I'm only saying that, if you begin to notice that he's trying to sabotage your efforts, then this might be the reason. Be aware of his anxieties, talk about them, reassure him and ask him to support you. After all, you do need all the help you can get because losing weight is very hard! One other thing you may need to remember: the closer you come to your target weight, the better you're beginning to feel about yourself, the better you're beginning to look, the more other people notice – the more reassurance he will need!

With weight gain, the sad thing is that a woman gets very

upset when her partner complains because she feels that she is still the same person inside, and that her appearance shouldn't matter. Unfortunately, however, sexual attraction has no logic and he may get turned off her because she doesn't look like the woman he fell in love with any more.

Growing older is different; it's something you do together and, provided you have taken note of the way you can keep a long-term relationship happy, then this shouldn't be a problem.

Men and women have very different needs and expectations some of which are explored in Chapters 8 and 13, Expectations: They Can Make Your Relationship Fail! and Men and Women: Are We Really So Different from Each Other?

Q: *How do you ask someone out without making it sound like a big deal?*

A: There are some do's and don'ts when it comes to asking people out. Let's start with the don'ts. The biggest don't is to ask, 'Are you doing anything Friday evening?' This is not an invitation, it's a trap, and most people tend to resent it. The other don't is to say, 'I really enjoyed talking with you, I'd like to meet you again some time.' The reason this is not a good invitation is that it isn't an invitation at all; it's too vague. The only thing the other person can say is, 'That would be nice.' Nothing will happen unless you make some specific suggestions, assuming that that's what you want.

A good way of asking someone out goes along the following lines: 'I really enjoyed talking with you. How about talking some more over a bite tomorrow at 12.30 at the MacDonald's around the corner from your office?' This is clear and specific and the other person knows exactly where they stand. They can say yes or they can say they'd like that, but not tomorrow, or not until one o'clock, or that they'd rather go to a Pizza Hut instead.

Taking the casual approach has a number of advantages. It's the easiest way to 'test the water' as it were, because if the other person declines after your other alternatives have not been taken up, you can withdraw gracefully without losing face. All you need to say is something like 'Oh, well! Perhaps some other time!' This kind of approach can certainly make the asking feel less daunting.

As a general rule, I would suggest that you keep the first invitation to a lunchtime snack or a coffee. Even a drink in the evening is better than making the first outing a full-scale dinner. First dates are hard enough without making it even harder by turning it into a special occasion. Both of you probably have expectations that are unrealistically high and which are bound to end in disappointment. You both feel you have to impress the other, be on your best behaviour, try hard to please or pretend to be cool. Making the first outing casual, and going somewhere non-threatening and low key, takes a lot of pressure off both of you. The idea is to get to know each other a little better and since you're not sure how you will get on together, then a brief first date is preferable to having to spend a whole evening together.

There are other reasons why it's better to keep the first date casual and informal. In the Nineties, men and women are often uncertain about what's expected of them and signals are sometimes still misunderstood. For example, there are men who have a fantasy of what a 'liberated' woman is like; if she takes the initiative and asks him out, he may believe that she also wants sex. Men, I urge you to forget this one as quickly as possible, because this kind of assumption can land you in real trouble. Pay attention to what the woman actually says and not what you think she may mean.

Another scenario involves the man who believes that the woman expects him to make a pass, otherwise she might think he doesn't consider her attractive, or that he's gay. Worrying about any of these things will spoil your first time out. But with lunch or an after-work drink, everything is much more clearcut: if you meet for lunch during the week, you both know that you have to get back to work. Similarly, if you meet for a drink in the evening, you know what to expect, so there is no awkwardness.

Taking it slowly and finding out about each other in safe surroundings and without pressure lets you both be yourself and that will save you a lot of disappointment, hurt feelings and frustration later on.

Another way to test the water is to make the next meeting a joint activity of mutual interest and, since you have spent some time talking and finding things out about each other, you may have discovered what this person is likely to enjoy doing. Choose something that allows you to talk and to get to know each other. For instance: 'Earlier on you mentioned that you enjoy watercolours. There is a Constable exhibition at the National Gallery for the next two weeks. Perhaps we could go together? When would suit you?'

Although the emphasis of this book is upon you being the one who takes the initiative, there will obviously be times when you will be at the receiving end of an invitation. If you can't make the date or time suggested, then offer an alternative provided, of course, that's what you want. Be careful how you word your response because people stop listening after they hear 'no'. The best way would be something along the lines of: 'I'd love to but I can't on Tuesday. How about Wednesday?'

Admitting that you feel a little nervous can work wonders for two reasons. First, because you may find, to your surprise, that once you admit to it, your nerves will actually disappear and, secondly, your partner may be greatly relieved to know that they weren't alone in feeling a little nervous, and that will reduce the tension.

Q: *Why do women always want to change a man once they've got him?*
(The women tend to become quite defensive when this question comes up.) Helping a man become the best he can possibly be is one of the ways women show their love and support for him. However, a man tends to see that as evidence that you're trying to change him because he isn't good enough.

A: The way out of this one is quite simple. Women, wait for him to ask you for help. You might find this hard to do especially because, if you offered your help and advice to one of your women friends without waiting to be asked, they would welcome it. Men don't. Being accepted unconditionally is one of their most important needs.

Q: *Why do women start making plans after we've been out a few times? Why do they make assumptions?*
(The women are surprised at this one because they thought they were going roughly in the same direction and at a similar pace as the men.)

A: This question suggests that sometimes a couple is out of synch in the things they want out of life and out of the relationship. Men and women tend to follow their own agendas but believe that they are both the same. However, research has shown that, while men fall in love quicker than women, once a woman has made up her mind (unconsciously, of course) that it's OK to fall in love with this particular man, she is then generally ready for commitment approximately twice as quickly as men. But, as my workshop shows, there are also men whose relationships have broken up because they were ready to settle down and have a family, while their partners weren't yet ready to commit themselves.

Clearly the problem comes when both assume that the other

wants the same things they do, without checking it out. (For more on the different needs and expectations of men and women, read Chapters 8 and 15.)

Q: *Why do women rehash the same old resentments again and again?*

A: Here's what some women have said:
- When I had a row with my ex-husband I always used to have the feeling that he would apologise for just about anything as long as it stopped the argument. It never resolved anything.
- I don't feel men understand why women get upset about things.
- Men seem to believe that, if you don't talk about something, it'll go away. It doesn't; it just gets worse.
- With my last boyfriend, I used to hope that, if I said it again and louder, he would hear me.

Men like to forget the unpleasantness and move on. They dislike raking over the issues because they believe that women expect them to admit that they screwed up yet again. The problem, however, is that unless the resentments are cleared up and resolved, they will remain and fester. That's what resentments are, old hurts, and people can only let go of them once they've stopped hurting. Otherwise, they will just keep coming up again and again every time there's a row. Men call it 'throwing everything at you, including the kitchen sink'.

TIPS
- Women, enjoy the date but don't spend the next week glued to the phone waiting for him to call.
- Women, do take the initiative and phone a man or ask him out. Without exception men say they would like it. Remember, confident is sexy!

- Men, don't make assumptions. If a woman asks you out, it doesn't mean that she wants anything else than to get to know you a little better.
- Women, don't let yourselves be talked into bed. Wait until you're ready.
- Women, don't expect men always to be ready for sex. Contrary to the myth, they're not sex machines.
- Women, remember that men expect women to offer to pay occasionally. Otherwise they will feel used. Treat them every once in a while.
- Men and women, when you ask someone out, keep it casual but be specific so there is no room for misunderstandings.
- Men and women, if you receive an invitation and you can't make a particular day, then word your response carefully. If you start with 'I can't' they'll stop listening to the 'because'. Say something like 'I'd love to but . . .' and offer an alternative.
- Men and women, if you're in doubt about how well you'll get along together, try to avoid making the first outing a dinner date. Test the water first with a lunchtime snack or an after work drink.
- Men and women, inviting someone to join you on an activity you are both likely to enjoy is a good way of asking someone out.
- Women, don't try to improve your man. Being accepted as he is is one of his greatest needs.
- Men and women, DO NOT TAKE EACH OTHER FOR GRANTED!

CHAPTER 13

Men and Women – Are We Really So Different from Each Other?

Have you ever thought your partner bloody-minded, unreasonable, perverse, downright weird, or maybe even from another planet altogether? Have you ever believed that he or she does it (whatever 'it' may be) on purpose, just to annoy you? If you have, then you're not alone!

I won't go into too much detail about the differences between men and women, because there are other books written especially about that, some of which you will find mentioned under 'Tips' below, but I thought it was important to start you thinking about this subject. That's because one of the ways we set ourselves up for disappointment is to assume that if our partner truly loved us, they would know what to do to make sure we feel loved and cherished, valued and understood. They would also know what they should not do to prevent us from feeling ignored, taken for granted and deeply wounded.

At the heart of this problem is the fact that men tend to love women the way they – the men – would like to be loved, while women tend to love men in the way they – the women – would like to be loved. And the sad thing is that the two often are very different.

Sandra came to see me very upset. She and Neil had only been together four months. From the very beginning he had told her that two of the things he loved about her were her kindness and her ability to listen to and understand him. She felt this was truly reciprocated and was convinced they were soulmates. Which is why she couldn't understand how they'd got themselves into this row. Apparently, he'd been having trouble at work but wouldn't go into details. Because she knows that it's no good to stifle your feelings, she'd tried, in her usual supportive and sympathetic way, to encourage him to share his problems, and confide in her. Instead of responding, he withdrew even more. The night before things had come to a head. He'd burst out: 'Get off my back!' As she was telling me about this, clearly distressed and obviously feeling helpless, it became clear to me that the more she pushed the more he retreated. 'I feel like he's keeping me at arm's length,' she told me. 'All I wanted to do was to be supportive. What have I done wrong?'

This is a classic example that highlights one of the many differences between men and women: the fact that men and women handle their frustrations and stresses differently.

Women need to talk things out. They tend to go on about 'what he said' and 'what she said' in return, and 'what happened then', and 'why do you think this was so?', and 'can you understand what must be going through his head?' This way of dealing with fears and anxieties helps them clarify their thinking, alleviate their feelings, and actually makes it much easier for them to deal with the situation. Unfortunately, however, while women friends understand and encourage this way of supporting one another (because, surely, that's the way people communicate when they care about each other, isn't it?), it usually irritates the hell out of men.

Men tend to deal with their frustrations and stresses in exactly the opposite way. They retreat. They need space to sort out their thoughts and feelings, and talking only gets in the way; not only does it frustrate them even more but it even delays their recovery. When women offer their active sympathy and try to encourage their men to talk about their feelings, they feel pushed, nagged, and even more stressed. So women, if you truly want to support your partner, back off! Give him space and, in his own good time when he feels able to do so because he has sorted things out in his head, he will come out of his shell – all sweetness and smiles, as if nothing had happened.

Once Sandra understood this difference, she no longer took it so personally and was able to give Neil the support he needed, in the way he needed it.

Unfortunately, nobody tells us about how men and women differ from each other, what we need to do to make our partner feel loved and cherished, supported and valued. Nobody tells us that the things that upset us about our partner, the things that make us believe that they're thoughtless, forgetful, or downright perverse and which clearly prove that they couldn't care less about us are, in fact, not proof at all. They're not being deliberately obnoxious, only fairly representative of the gender as a whole. For us women, the biggest mistake we can make is to expect men to be like our women friends. For men it is to expect that their women should – as Professor Higgins in *My Fair Lady* put it – 'be more like a man'.

I know, I know, you're going to tell me about your man, and how he is as supportive as the best of your women friends, and how he tunes into your feelings before you've even understood them yourself. Or your girlfriend or wife who knows exactly when to leave you alone, and when not to. You're absolutely right, and I know this from my own personal experience, but these are exceptions. There are far too many of you out there convinced that you've chosen the wrong partner. I want to say to you, loudly and clearly, that men and women are different from one another. It is important to be aware of at least some of our innate differences so we can become more tolerant and understanding of each other, so we can stop taking things personally and, what's even more important, so we can recognise that we need to find out how to love our partner so that they feel truly cherished – rather than assuming that their way is the same as ours. This realisation will go a long way to save us a lot of hurt, disappointment, frustration, confusion and misunderstandings.

If you've been experiencing these differences day in, day out, year in, year out throughout your relationship and have interpreted them as proof of the ill will of your partner, I'd like you to get away from these kinds of conversations – if you can call them that . . .

WOMAN: If you really loved me . . .

- you'd listen to me more
- you'd spend more time with me instead of your horrible friends
- you'd support me when I'm down in the dumps.

MAN: Look who's talking! If you really loved me . . .

- you wouldn't nag and complain the whole time
- you'd make love to me when I'm feeling horny instead of having yet another one of your headaches
- you wouldn't go on at me when I want to watch the telly.

By the time you get to this stage, a lot of water will have gone under the bridge. Obviously, I don't know all your grievances but maybe, by the time you reach the end of the chapter, there may be a chink of light that will show you the way out.

Let's start with the basics: Men and women think, feel and act differently. And that's not all. They also differ in the things that they regard as important, and in their perceptions, expectations, assumptions and goals. Some of them may have to do with the basic differences that exist between the genders, while others will have been influenced by the way we've been brought up, Hollywood movies, romantic novels, pornography and television. When you think about it, it's a miracle we

126

manage to get along even as well as we do!

Here are some examples of how men and women differ from one another, not only to help us all understand each other a little better but also to give us a better chance to establish healthier, happier and more fulfilling relationships.

Talking

EXAMPLE 1
What's the purpose of talking? The purpose for women is usually to come closer to people without having a specific end goal in mind, while for men it's usually to exchange information. Men like to get to the point.

EXAMPLE 2
Men tend to be more literal than women, because women are prone to absolutes as in 'you always', 'you never', 'everybody always', 'nobody ever', and so on. Men think they mean exactly what they say and become resentful. Generally, men tend to say exactly what they mean (unless they feel angry or hurt in which case they tend to clam up), while women look for the hidden message along the lines of 'If I'd said that what I would really mean is . . .'

EXAMPLE 3
Women are used since childhood to talk about feelings with their girlfriends. Men have had no such experience. In fact, men are usually uncomfortable talking about their feelings, not because they don't have them, but because talking about them is like speaking a different language. It's awkward, it's difficult – and it takes time.

EXAMPLE 4
Sometimes the problem is not what you say to a man but what you don't say. Too often women fail to spell out exactly what they want, expecting men to read their minds. Men, as a rule,

want to get on with finding a solution, while women prefer to express their feelings first. What often happens is that a man may leap in with advice before the woman has finished telling her story. Then she gets upset and complains, 'You're not listening! You never listen!' He feels hurt and angry. 'Not listening? You've been talking about this problem for the last hour and here I am, trying to help you solve it! What do you want from me?'

A way out of this one is for women to preface the whole story with 'I'm going to tell you about a problem I have at work. You don't have to solve it, all you have to do is listen and commiserate.'

EXAMPLE 5

Goodwill plays a big part in improving communications between the two of you. If your partner reacts in a defensive way when you say things in what you may describe as a 'completely non-confrontational or non-aggressive manner', don't assume that that's just his problem.

Good communication has little to do with intention and everything to do with perception. When what you say is understood in the way that you mean it, then harmony will generally follow, as long as there's goodwill between you. If there are frequent misunderstandings between the two of you, then you will have to look not only at what you say but also at how you say it, your choice of words and, especially, the tone of your voice which can totally change the meaning of your words.

Getting to know one another

When it comes to making friends and forming relationships, there are even more pitfalls. Women show their interest by asking questions and really listening. Men don't do that very often. In fact, women often complain that men show little interest in them, and that they feel as if they are expected to carry the conversation. They say that men 'never' ask them questions about themselves. Both men and women alike interpret being asked questions about themselves as a sign of interest. Women have learned to do this from an early age, men haven't.

So, men, if you really want to make a good impression, ask women questions about themselves and really listen to their answers. This is a very good way to make them feel valued, interesting and important, and will bring you rewards beyond your wildest dreams!

Phoning

EXAMPLE 1
She tends to think that, once they've started going out together, he'll call her every day, if not more often. He sometimes gets involved in other things and forgets. It's nothing personal.

EXAMPLE 2
If he rings after not having called for several days, she will give him a frosty response. 'That'll teach him not to take me for granted!' As far as he's concerned, there's nothing to learn and he can't understand why she's so frosty. He decides she's either completely unreasonable or playing games – probably both.

Intimacy

EXAMPLE 1
For her it means talking and sharing secrets. For him it means sex or just being with her. She sees that as evidence that he's not interested in her any more.

EXAMPLE 2
She thinks intimacy means spending as much time together as

possible. He needs space. She feels hurt because she believes that's proof that he doesn't love her any more.

Making improvements

How can you go about making changes? Here's a two-pronged approach:

1. With a pencil, draw a horizontal line. The ends represent the two extremes: on the left, total distance and, on the right, you're practically sitting on top of each other the whole time. A comfortable degree of intimacy for women is about two-thirds towards the right-hand side, give or take a little. Men fluctuate. They tend to go backwards and forwards along the continuum which confuses women no end. Men are more likely to withdraw *after* a wonderfully intimate time together, which is particularly hurtful for women because they really haven't got a clue about what they've done wrong. (Have you noticed that, whenever something goes wrong in a relationship, women always wonder what *they* did wrong?) Too much closeness for men is overwhelming and they're afraid of being swallowed up and taken over. So, distancing themselves is a way of reasserting their individuality and independence.

The solution is to leave him alone, don't question him about what's wrong (he would probably have a hard time putting it into words), or whether you have said or done anything to upset him.

2. This suggestion is based on the fact that you can't change people by wishing, nagging or complaining 'You never talk to me!' Instead, act as you'd like him to act. In parallel with backing off a little, you can continue to show an interest in him. Every once in a while, create relaxed opportunities – not too long ones – where you can ask him questions and really listen to his answers. Whatever you do, don't rush him or force him into it – and, above all, be patient.

Here is another tip for women. Sometimes, men take a while to reply. This does not mean that they haven't heard you; what it usually means is that they need to think before they can answer, and they take their time so you may need to get used to long silences in order not to interrupt their train of thought.

Start as you mean to go on. Later on it may be harder to shift – though not impossible if you have a lot of love and patience – because people get used to ways of doing things.

Love and commitment

EXAMPLE 1
Men tend to fall in love twice as fast as women, while women, once they've made up their minds about the suitability of a particular man, will tend to be ready for commitment roughly twice as fast as men.

EXAMPLE 2
Men are often afraid of commitment – even when it's furthest from the woman's mind. This is particularly true in the earlier stages of the relationship and has nothing to do with the woman and everything to do with timing and the man's needs at that particular juncture. It's an inner fear of the unspoken expectation that 'one thing will lead to another', especially if things go really well.

Timing is the magic ingredient that can make a relationship flow – or not. Sometimes it may literally be a case of 'right person – wrong time'.

Vanessa came to one of my workshops and, when a question came up about how men and women perceived the whole issue of commitment, she offered the following story. She had met Guy and they both got along really well. Several months later they went away for a weekend together and, in her own words 'It was absolutely smashing. And not just for me. I know it was just as good for him. Next thing I know, I get this message on my answer machine saying that he just wasn't ready for commitment. I never said anything about commitment! What on earth happened?'

Well, believe it or not, the problem was that things were 'too good' and the internal pressure was on. That's what prompted him to make his escape. I'm sure this will sound strange to you women but, if the men in that workshop were anything to go by, it will ring bells for lots of you chaps out there. Running away is an extreme example of fear of commitment; a more common reaction is putting things off and refusing to make a decision one way or another.

I'm sorry I have no magic answer for you women. All I can say is that it's up to you to decide if you want to hang around until he's ready to decide.

Sex

For him, having sex when he feels horny is often proof that she loves him. If she feels pressured, she may end up feeling used and resentful.

Love words

For her, hearing him say 'I love you' is proof of love. For him, the proof is in the fact that he's there. 'Waddya mean, do I love you? I'm here, ain't I?'

More proofs of loving

She may buy him a little gift or send him a funny card. He may wash her car or take out the rubbish. The tragedy is when neither recognises these gestures for what they are and both end up feeling unloved.

True love

She thinks that doing everything for him is what will make him feel loved. A great housekeeper, a terrific Mum to him and to his children, she recognises his talent and wants him to be the best he could be. She may even tie his ties and shoelaces for him, cut the meat into small pieces and wipe his mouth! I've heard countless women whose partners have left them say to me: 'I've done everything for him and this is the thanks I get!'

He begs to differ: she nags all the time, criticises him constantly, never wants to have sex with him, wants a super-hero and shows him in lots of different ways that he simply isn't good enough for her. He feels unwanted and lonely. And, no, he isn't a wimp.

Women, most men don't want you to do everything for them! They're not helpless children – not unless you taught them to become helpless. If you don't know what your partner wants – and assume you don't – ask! Better safe than sorry . . . P.S. This goes for you guys as well!

There is a sting in the tail for women who love their men to death – at least the death of their soul – but such women don't see this at all. They see their love as selfless and generous – which is how they themselves would like to be loved in return – and when the men don't reciprocate the women feel cheated and resentful.

Work

He still feels that he has to be the provider; that it's up to him to look after her and the family so he works day and night to give her the best of everything. She doesn't want everything: she wants him. As a result, he feels unappreciated and she feels lonely.

The meaning of life, the universe and everything

Hers: Having a happy love life
His: Being respected for his achievements.

We could ask ourselves why we are so different from each other but that's not really important – that's just the way we are. None of it means that one way of being is better or worse than the other, that one is insensitive and thoughtless while the other is manipulative and emotional. We can become very creative in the way we label people and that is a very dangerous game. Couldn't we just try to remember that we simply come from different places and are, therefore, well, different?

If we can learn to say what we mean and mean what we say, so there are no misunderstandings, rather than expecting our partner to read between the lines; to ask for what we want and need instead of somehow expecting them 'to know'; and to listen carefully with an open mind and an open heart, then I think we have more than a sporting chance to have happy and fulfilling relationships.

TIPS
- Men and women differ from each other in the ways they act, think, feel and communicate as well as in their perceptions, expectations, assumptions and goals. Being aware of these differences will give you a better chance to establish healthier, happier and more fulfilling personal relationships.
- For more insights into the differences between men and women, read
  i) *That's Not What I Meant!* by Deborah Tannen
  ii) *You Just Don't Understand!* by Deborah Tannen
  iii) *Men Are from Mars, Women Are from Venus* by Dr John Gray
  iv) *Why They Don't Call When They Say They Will* by Dr Joy Browne
- Don't assume men and women want to be treated as you would if you were them. You're not. If what you do doesn't work, instead of effecting a wounded retreat, ask them what they need from you.
- Men, to show your interest at whatever stage of the conversation, friendship or relationship, ask women questions about themselves and listen very carefully to their answers. You will gain major rewards!

- Women, don't let silences throw you after you've asked a man a question. Men sometimes need to take their time to think things through before responding.
- Women, be prepared to listen to all of men's feelings, not just the so-called 'acceptable' ones. Men usually respond with loyalty to unconditional acceptance.
- Men, women do too!
- Respect each other's confidences and never use them against the other in a row.

CHAPTER 14

To Make Contact . . . Use Your Eyes

Making good eye contact is probably one of the most important social skills because people make all sorts of assumptions about the kind of person we are on the basis of whether or not we look at them. If we have difficulty looking at others we will, at best, be regarded as nervous, tense, evasive and lacking in confidence and, at worst, as shifty, as having something to hide, and perhaps even as dishonest. On the other hand, if we're good at making eye contact we will be seen not only as friendly and confident but even as more attractive.

Our eyes can be our greatest allies because eye contact is one of the cues we can use not only to initiate contact but also to continue showing our interest in someone. There are other clues to indicate – or recognise – interest, such as physical proximity and touch so, if you want to use all your 'weapons', then standing a shade closer than normal to your quarry and touching them lightly while continuing to hold their gaze and speaking in a soft tone of voice, will have a devastating effect. However, don't rush out to try this just yet – you're not quite ready for it. First you have to read Chapter 21, The Power of Touch.

If eye contact can have such a dramatic effect, why do we waste its power? The reason is that there's more to making eye contact than meets the eye. If it were just a matter of technique, then we would all be doing it really well as a matter of course – and we aren't. To understand some of what happens, we have to re-visit the basics.

Whenever we meet someone we're attracted to, the first thing we do is we look at them. The idea is simply to attract attention. But then, suddenly, out of the blue, we become extremely self-conscious, especially if that person has really taken our fancy – our brain stops functioning altogether, just when we need it most! At that point we start thinking about everything we imagine is wrong with us. Our feelings of inadequacy take over with the belief that nobody that gorgeous could possibly be the least bit interested in us. We wish we had worn the green dress instead of the blue one; that we had washed our hair or put make-up on; or we're suddenly conscious of our fat thighs or big bottom or small breasts. Men may wonder if their tie is straight; if their pot-belly shows; whether their socks match; or they worry about their little bald patch which is invisible to everybody except them. Whether we realise it or not, the message we're sending out is loud and clear: 'I wonder what you think of me?' or 'You probably think I'm boring.' And believe me, it shows.

But, stop! What you have in front of you is not some unobtainable god or goddess but an ordinary human being just like you, someone with hopes and dreams, anxieties and fears, who wants to make friends, who occasionally has self-doubts, and who from time to time also gets rejected.

So, the way forward is really simple enough although in the beginning, it may take a bit of an effort. What you do is you try to forget about yourself and how you're feeling, and think instead of how interested you are in the other person. This is not as easy as it sounds, I know, and will require you to undertake a major shift in the way you think but it is absolutely critical if you want to start making contact with people. The irony is that most people feel just as vulnerable as you do, however confident they may appear to be and however attractive they may look to you. Inside they're thinking about their own thighs, bottoms, pot-bellies or bald patches, and wondering what impression they're making on you. Remember this

138

when you feel an attack of insecurity coming on.

Sam is a case in point. Ever since he became aware of his little bald patch, he has been feeling extremely self-conscious. Things got so bad that he even began to believe that it was the first and only thing people noticed about him, and he started to avoid going out. Sam came to see me because he was feeling lonely and didn't know what to do about it. When I suggested that he was becoming very self-centred he was shocked because he saw himself as a kind person – which he was. However, after a while, he began to realise that other people were most probably feeling just as nervous as he. It took him a little time and quite a bit of effort to shift his way of thinking, but he finally succeeded in making the conscious decision to stop worrying about how nervous he felt and focus instead on other people, trying to make them feel more at ease.

When I saw him again, he was all smiles, his confidence restored. He had been invited to join the committee in charge of organising social events at his local sports club. Sam's story illustrates very vividly not only the power our thoughts have on the way we behave, but also that we can decide to change the record in our heads.

Connecting with our eyes can sometimes be difficult for a number of reasons. One reason is that it can make us feel uncomfortable, another is that our feelings about ourselves can get in the way of the message we want to convey, so we either send conflicting messages or misinterpret the meaning of another person's look. The good news, though, is that there's hope!

Interest or attraction can be friendly as well as sexual. Let's start with what is going on in our heads when we initiate eye contact.

Most people don't realise how much impact their thoughts have on how they are seen by others. This is because what they think affects how they feel and therefore how they act. So, to convey the message you want to convey, you first have to be clear about what is going on in your head. If you think it will help, change or edit your thoughts; then let them show in your eyes when you look at the person that attracted your interest. For example, if you're thinking: 'What a great-looking hunk!', or 'What a terrific body!' (or both), it will generally show in your eyes, unless you choose to censor that thought. If you're sure that that's the message you want to send, then that's fine. But be careful, especially if you're a man, because women generally dislike lecherous leers. On the other hand, I must confess that I've never heard men complaining about women leering at them – at least, not yet!

If you're experimenting with different types of thoughts, you might like to start with something friendly such as, 'You look like a fun person, I'd like to get to know you', or 'You look like a really interesting person', then let your eyes show it. This is something else you can practise in front of the mirror in the privacy of your own home.

But, as you're probably beginning to realise, the other person may not be certain what your glance means so you have to help them. One way is by doing a double-take which helps the other person to be sure that you are looking at them – and not at someone standing behind them.

A woman friend was recently going through a minor crisis of confidence. Out of the blue – or so it seemed to me – she burst out one day, 'Nobody finds me attractive. I can't remember the last time a man tried to chat me up.' I was completely taken aback because of the many times I had noticed how men looked at her, occasionally sending signals that required some sort of response before the approach was made but to which my friend was totally oblivious. From the man's point of view, approaching someone who appears not to be in the slightest bit interested is asking for punishment. When I reminded her of the times I had commented that such and such seemed interested in her, she simply had no idea what I was talking about.

140

The point of the story is that we're often totally absorbed in our thoughts, too busy to notice what's going on around us so, every once in a while, we have to 'resurface' and pay attention to the people around us. From the discussions in my workshop, two things have become clear to me:

1. We don't notice or recognise another person's interest in us simply because we're not tuning in.
2. We misinterpret the meaning of the glance because of the way we feel about ourselves. This works along the lines of 'If I don't particularly like myself, how could anybody else?' Is that masochism or what!

So many wasted opportunities! But no longer. To show someone that you're interested in them, this is what you do:

1. Look at them for a fraction longer than you would someone who leaves you cold. If you notice that the other person seems uncomfortable, look away to break the tension, and then do a double-take to confirm your interest.
2. At the same time, smile at them to indicate warmth, interest and liking and to look friendly. If you don't smile, they may feel threatened, stared at, or as if they are under a microscope.

So smile a warm and friendly smile, and go over to the other person. What happens next is discussed in great detail in the next chapter, 'Do You Come Here Often?' and Other Openings to Avoid.

TIPS
- Focus on the other person – not on your imagined flaws.
- Think the kind of thoughts you want people to read in your eyes, for example, how nice, interesting, fun and attractive you think they are.

- When you see someone you'd like to meet, look at them a fraction longer than usual. If they seem uncomfortable, break off your gaze, but do a double-take.
- When you glance at people, do smile at them with real warmth. This will soften your expression, and make you come across as friendly, confident, approachable, and attractive to boot!

CHAPTER 15

'Do You Come Here Often?' and Other Openings to Avoid

Up to this point the kind of eye contact we have been talking about assumed that you were some distance away. Now we've got to the stage where you've made eye contact with someone you find really attractive, you smiled at them, you told them with your eyes that you would really like to get to know them, and they have indicated with their eyes that they would like to get to know you too.

The next step is to say something that will draw that person into a conversation. Approaching a stranger and speaking to them causes people a lot of anxiety. I bet many of you still hope for that magic first sentence, some sort of 'Open sesame!' that will open the doors to conversation, love and friendship. Unfortunately – or fortunately – people are much too complex and too unpredictable, and there is no foolproof way of approaching someone. In fact, most people don't like chat-up lines; they think they're tacky.

Even so, most people still worry about having to think of something witty, funny, or interesting to say to catch someone's attention. If you're one of those people, then I have good news for you. Research into this topic has shown that, unless the approach is in some way crude or offensive, it really doesn't matter what you say. Aren't you relieved? The only thing that matters is that you manage to hook them into talking with you, and you're off!

You know how people make fun of the English because they're always talking about the weather? Well, even something as boring as the good old English weather has proved to work in getting people to talk to one another. So, if you're really desperate, you can always fall back on the weather, although I hope that after reading this chapter you will come up with something a little more creative.

You don't need to think of anything clever or witty, the only thing you need to do is to show how interested you are in the other person. And do you know why? It's because that is intensely flattering.

Stop for a moment and ask yourself, what was it about that person that caught your attention? What made you focus on him or her instead of on anybody else? It might, for example, have been their lovely smile, the way they dress, a special accessory, a brooch, pin or badge they are wearing. Perhaps you noticed they have really nice eyes, they look like a fun person to know or you heard them say something that struck you as interesting.

Once you have decided what you particularly liked about them, keep it simple especially if you're the kind of person for whom just walking up to someone is a major achievement. Start by introducing yourself: 'Hello, I'm Tom Wright, your new neighbour', or 'I'm Jennifer Stubbs of Accounts', or 'I'm Louise Green, I'm a researcher', or 'I'm Richard Gordon, a friend of Sandie and Bob', and then go on to what you actually want to say to that person, for example:

- 'You look like such a fun person, I wanted to come over and meet you'
- 'I overheard you say . . . which I thought was interesting because . . .' (and follow this with an open question)
- 'I see you're reading X – what do you think of it?'
- 'That's a striking belt you're wearing, where did you find it?'

- 'You look like you've just come back from a sunny holiday. Where did you get that tan?'
- 'Of all the people in the room, I wanted to come over and chat *you* up' (said with a smile! A woman is more likely to get away with this one)
- 'That's an interesting accent. I've been trying to place it but I can't. Can you help me out?'
- 'I've been making bets with my friend about your accent. I say you come from Australia and he said you come from London. Who wins?' (It doesn't matter if this sounds a little weird: It might just get them laughing and break the ice!)

If you feel more creative, you can try something like:

- 'If you could wave a magic wand and do anything in the world, what would you like to do?'
- 'Imagine you are eighty-five years old. What would you regret not having done?'

If you see someone in the street that appeals to you, you might try asking them for directions which require more than an 'Oh! That's just around the corner!' kind of answer.

Here's one for men to try; but this is something really adventurous and needs to be carried off with grace and confidence. If you see a woman sitting by herself, bring her a flower (just one, not a bunch), and say something like 'I had the sudden urge to offer you this flower. I hope you don't mind but, if you do, tell me and I will go away.' (Be sure to apologise and withdraw if she doesn't react as you hoped.)

Just to balance things out, this is one for women to try. This approach consists of two stages:

Stage 1: Imagine you see a man sitting by himself and you really like the look of him. Go over to him with complete confidence, stretch out your hand and say, 'Hi! I'm Christina

Fenchurch. What's your name?' The man may hesitate for a moment but he will take your outstretched hand and shake it, mostly because it's an automatic response. If he gives you his name, say 'Hello (name), it's nice to meet you. Well, I've got to go now. Bye!' Now turn and walk firmly away, preferably until you're out of sight.

Stage 2: Walk back to him and say with a big smile, 'Bob? How nice to see you again! How are you?' If he has any sense of humour, chances are he will burst out laughing – and you're in.

If you can't see yourself using either of these bold approaches, stick to the basic suggestions I gave you before. You can try the light-hearted approach, or you can be more formal. Whichever you choose, don't suddenly start using a style that is completely different from your own, because not only will you find it hard to carry off and sustain, but people will have trouble working out the real you and may end up feeling confused and uncomfortable.

Sometimes all you need is something totally innocuous, just to test the water without taking too much of a risk to see how the other person responds. Getting people to talk with you need not be a major enterprise. Conversations can start by simply saying something pleasant, such as 'Are you having a good time?', or 'I notice your glass is empty, would you like a refill?' or, if you're travelling in the lift together. 'Hi! Do you work in this building?' Just express a genuine interest in that person and things will begin to happen.

Remember, what you say is less important than the fact you actually say something and make contact. The good news is that, the more you do it, the more comfortable you will feel about the whole business of approaching people and getting them to talk with you.

Another reason you don't need to worry about what to say is

that there are, in fact, really only three basic subjects to talk about. You can say something about the other person, something connected with yourself, or you might comment on the place where you are; you might even combine the three. For example, 'Apart from Chris and Timothy, our hosts, I don't know anybody else. Do you know many people here?', or 'I do enjoy coming to these conferences, because you get a chance of meeting interesting people. Are you a regular visitor to these events?'

These examples start with a comment about the situation, in this case the cocktail party and the conference, respectively, which is then followed by a question to give the person a chance to answer. Usually, the best way is to ask an *open question*, that is a question that starts with 'How . . .?', 'What did you think of . . .?', 'Why . . .?', 'Tell me about . . .'. These are the kind of questions that can't be answered with just a 'yes' or a 'no'. Or you can start with a *closed question*, that is the kind that generates brief and specific information, for example: 'Are . . .?' 'Do . . .?', 'Who . . .?', 'When . . .?', 'Which . . .?', 'Where . . .?', and follow that with an open question.

Here are more examples:

- (at a concert) 'You look like you're enjoying the music. Do you come to concerts often? Who is your favourite composer?'
- (at a regular meeting) 'Hello, I haven't seen you here before. Are you a member or a guest?'
- (on a course or seminar) 'That speaker gave some really good ideas. Which did you find the most useful?'

Another way to start a conversation is to give an opinion. If you decide to go for this approach, make sure your opinions are of the positive kind. The negative ones like 'What dreadful weather!', 'Isn't the music loud!', 'The food isn't much to write home about' can put people off. Making any kind of factual statement isn't particularly helpful, unless you follow it with a question, because the other person can't hook into it. Whichever approach you decide to go for, remember that the purpose is to get a conversation off the ground.

If you are not used to taking the initiative, you may find that in the beginning results are a bit uneven, or that you may say something that, looking back, you wish you hadn't. It happens to all of us. Don't be too hard on yourself. There's always another time, another place, another person. If you happen to come out with something that, on reflection, you thought sounded a bit silly, instead of mumbling an apology and slinking away, try turning it to your advantage and say something like, 'Oh God! Did I really say that?! Could we please forget it and start again?' You'd be surprised how refreshing a genuinely friendly approach is. So, whatever you do, don't give up!

When you do ask a question, listen very carefully to the reply, and try to relate to it. That will give you the handle you need to respond and to get the conversation off the ground.

As the conversation develops, the other person will also ask you questions. Unfortunately, what often happens when people feel nervous is that they tend to blurt out the first thing that comes into their head. This is the 'foot in mouth' syndrome which can cause you great embarrassment at the time. So, when someone asks you a question, pause, breathe in, engage your brain before you open your mouth, and only reply when you feel ready. For more on how to develop more interesting conversations, read Chapter 18: What Do You Say After You Say 'Hello'?

Here's another tip you might find helpful. If you decide that you want to widen your social circle, the more you know about what's going on in the world the more interesting your conversations will be, and you will also be able to relate even better to all kinds of people. Read the current affairs sections in the papers, listen to the news, open yourself up to different views and opinions, become an expert in your profession and/or your hobby, challenge your own attitudes by reflecting on your beliefs and whether, in the light of your experience, they're still valid. You'd be surprised how much mental and emotional 'baggage' we carry around that is long out of date. Open up your mind, get rid of the cobwebs and let in the light!

Research into what attracts people to one another has demonstrated that we are attracted to people who show that they like us and are interested in us. Think about this for a moment because this is really important.

> WE WARM TO PEOPLE WHO SHOW THAT
> THEY GENUINELY LIKE US.

Men and women who are really good at attracting people do exactly that. They take the trouble to express their liking and interest in the other person in a number of different ways. Some can be non-verbal, such as focusing all their attention on the other person, listening without letting themselves be distracted by what is going on around them, leaning closer towards them (an attentive posture), and touching them lightly. They also express their liking for the other person in words. All this is extraordinarily powerful because deep down we are all insecure, and looking for approval and appreciation. When someone lets us know that they like us, it means much more to us than a simple pleasantry, it's like giving food to a starving person. Remember everyone wants to be liked, appreciated, approved of and accepted.

One of the most important habits you can develop is to make a conscious effort to look for attractive qualities in every person you meet, and the exercise in Chapter 1 will help you do this.

Sadly, we often hesitate to tell people that we like them for a variety of reasons. Sometimes it's because we operate on a 'no news is good news' way of dealing with people, so the thought that they might want – let alone need – to hear it, doesn't even enter our minds. Another reason may be that we believe that 'It's just not done. They'll think I'm pushy or downright weird.' Here, too, our habitual thoughts get in the way. We worry about *what they might think of us* instead of forgetting about ourselves and focusing on the other person.

Another reason why we are reluctant to reveal our affection, or even liking, is that we're afraid that if we do we might scare people off. People may wonder why you are telling them, or what, if anything, you expect from them in return. To be fair, it does depend on how it's done and the difference is subtle. If you express your feelings conditionally, that is, if you hope to get something in return, then they're likely to feel pressured, but if you tell them freely, without expecting anything back, then they will feel good about it. For example, if you say: 'I really like you. When will I see you again?', they might feel pressured, especially if you say it too soon but, if you say: 'Do you know, it's been ages since I last met someone with whom I had such a good time talking', that's unconditional appreciation, and it will leave you both feeling really good about yourselves. Then, later on, you might like to ask them out though it needn't automatically follow. In Chapter 12, Why Do Men? Why Do Women? Questions and Answers you will find some tips on how to do this.

As with all the ideas in this book, you will need to practise this but I urge you to develop the habit of taking this tiny risk because people who express their liking or, indeed, their affection tend to be very good at attracting others. It would be unrealistic to expect that this will work every time because different approaches work for different people at different times. We all have our own preferences, so there isn't any one single approach that works with everybody. But if you get into the habit of approaching people remember we're all individuals, not types, and we don't want to be fed a line.

What we do like – always – is genuine interest. Remember that and you will be pleasantly surprised at the results. So don't wait for others to make a move! Take control and make things happen!

TIPS

- You don't need to show how witty, funny or interesting you are to get someone to talk with you. The only thing you need to do is to show that you're genuinely interested in the other person.
- The more informed you are, the more interesting your conversations will be. Open your mind to the world around you.
- Everyone has a deep need to know that they are liked and appreciated. Show them you do but do it without expecting anything in return.
- Try out the various different ways of approaching people until you find one that feels comfortable for you. Keep it simple but keep looking for opportunities wherever you are.

CHAPTER 16

How to Avoid
Being a Bore

Being seen as a bore will be the kiss of death to your ambitions of building a more exciting social life. We tend to avoid bores like the plague and being considered one is regarded as one of the worst possible sins. The problem is that, while we all recognise a bore at ten paces, it's much more difficult to recognise boring characteristics in ourselves. We all like to think we're fun, witty, amusing and interesting – all the time. Reality may be slightly different. Almost everyone has some boring qualities so, if you want to widen your social circle, it would be useful to find out how you affect people. Only then will you be able to do something about it.

Studies have been made into what qualities people regard as boring and, to help you assess which, if any, you may possess, do the following exercise. First do it on your own, and be as honest as possible! To help you with the questionnaire, think back. Has anybody ever made any of these comments about you? Perhaps more than one person? After you have done it, ask one or two friends you trust to complete the same questionnaire with you in mind. You may be surprised (pleasantly or otherwise . . .).

Take a blank sheet of paper, write down the numbers of each question with your answer – often, sometimes or never.

(a) i) Do you show little interest in others and drone on and on about yourself or your hobby horse?

    ii) Do you talk only about superficial things?

   iii) Do you tend to monopolise the conversation?

(b) i) Do you try too hard to impress?

    ii) Do you name-drop, talk about your prestigious job in some glamorous industry?

   iii) Do you talk about how much you earn or about your impressive sports car? In short, do you show off?

(c) i) Do you try too hard to please?

    ii) Do you try too hard to be funny?

(d) i) Do you make jokes which no one regards as funny except yourself?

    ii) Do they tend to be sexist, racist or otherwise offensive?

   iii) Do you regard other people as having no sense of humour?

(e) i) Do you repeat the same stories and jokes frequently?

(f) i) Do you use too much slang or the same expression again and again, such as 'you know' or 'As the actress said to the Bishop'?

    ii) Do you use bad language?

(g) i) Do you avoid looking at people, have a rather unemotional facial expression, or smile only rarely?

(h) i) Do you speak in a monotonous voice?

    ii) Do you speak too slowly or too fast?

   iii) Is your speech unclear? (If you're not sure, record your voice and listen to yourself.)

(i) i) Do you only see the dark side of things, and are you always complaining about the state of the world and your problems?

(j) i) Do you fail to express opinions, always sitting on the fence?

 ii) Do you always agree with everybody else so that people end up thinking you have no views of your own?

It's highly unlikely that any one person would have most of these traits at any one time. It would be extremely unfortunate if they did but even then all would not be lost. As a rule, what makes people behave in a tactless and insensitive manner is either that they don't realise they do, or because they have low self-esteem. Even – or especially – those who continually boast about how clever they are! They tend to want people to think well of them without realising that their behaviour has the opposite effect. Most people with boring qualities like the ones highlighted above have no idea how they come across. The first thing you need to do is become aware of your own bad habits – that's all they are. The good news is that bad habits can be changed, so here are some ideas about what you can do:

• Try to forget about what other people might think of you and focus instead on them. Read Chapters 14 and 19, To Make Contact . . . Use Your Eyes and Listening: The Ultimate Aphrodisiac.
• If you find out that your voice is expressionless and monotonous, or that you speak too slowly or too fast, you have several options. You might find it helpful to join your local amateur dramatics, to go to a voice coach, or to enrol in one of the many public-speaking courses available. Ask your librarian. They are usually very helpful. Depending on which route you choose, talk to various

voice coaches and trainers to find out how they could help before choosing one.

- If you find it hard to look people in the eye, work at it because, as you now know, making good eye contact is an extremely important social skill.

- If your facial expression is impassive and unresponsive, people may regard you as cold and indifferent. It's irrelevant what you feel like inside if you don't allow anyone to see it. Practising different emotions in front of the mirror is a good first step. Try practising fascinated interest, excitement, being thrilled at a friend's good news, genuine concern for someone, sadness, anxiety, and so on. In the beginning, you may find it difficult to differentiate emotions so try to exaggerate and really ham it up! After all, no one can see you.

  Both amateur dramatics and public-speaking courses will also help with this because they will show you how to match what you say with how you say it, and you will then discover that people will find you much more attractive. Make sure you discuss this as well before you make your final choice of route.

- If you realise that you have a negative and pessimistic disposition, you need to work on this urgently. Not only do you drag yourself down with your constant negativity and pessimism, but you also drag down everyone else around you. Negative people are draining and they should wear a health warning on their forehead! Read Chapter 25, The Art of Being Happy.

  A good way of starting is to decide to go through a whole day without complaining about one single thing and finding at least three positive things to be pleased about. Then extend this gradually and persevere until it becomes a habit. Also, read Chapter 24, How to Care for Yourself: The Magic of Self-Esteem.

- If you are one of those people who try to be all things to all people because you want to be liked at all costs, then I have bad news for you: it doesn't work. People tend to distrust 'yes' people because they can't make them out, and they have a difficult time working out where they really stand with them.

Develop your own views and opinions. Challenge your values and your attitudes. Discover what is important to you, what you feel strongly about. Become passionate about something, ideally something that involves both your heart and your mind. Broaden your interests. Listen carefully to what people say, then reflect on it, decide whether or not you agree with it, and why or why not. That doesn't mean you should ram your views down everybody's throat. It does mean, however, that you can say,' I'm not sure I agree with that because . . .' and then go on to explain. You will be a lot more interesting to talk with.

If you feel anxious about letting go of your bad habits, don't worry. You don't have to drop them all at once; just work on each, one at the time. But I do urge you to try because people cannot develop a genuine conversation, much less a relationship with people who hide behind a wall of defences and who are practically impossible to get close to.

TIPS
- Stop wondering what others think of you. Forget about yourself and focus instead on the other person.
- Find out if there is a local amateur dramatics society in your area, find a voice coach or enrol on a public-speaking course. It will do wonders for your voice, your facial expression, your body language and, as a bonus, for your self-confidence.
- If you prefer, start by practising different facial expressions in front of the mirror.

- Spend a whole day without complaining about one single thing and find at least three positive things to be happy about. Then gradually extend this for longer and longer periods until it becomes a habit.
- Trying to be liked by everybody doesn't work. Become passionate about something that engages both your heart and your mind, and develop your own views and opinions.

CHAPTER 17

How to Recognise the Right Partner for You

Do you believe that somewhere on this planet lives one kindred spirit whom you're destined to meet and spend the rest of your life with, happily, in blissful harmony, for ever and ever? This may shock you: he or she does not exist. And that's not all. There are many people out there with whom you could happily spend the rest of your life if – and only if – you do your homework. If this sounds horribly unromantic, I make no apologies. The 'love is blind' school of thought has been shown up for what it is: a painfully misleading fairy tale.

Unfortunately, as statistics of divorce and broken relationships show, we seem to invest more time in choosing the right car or the right washing machine than we do in choosing the person with whom we hope to share the rest of our lives. I think we've got our priorities a little upside down, wouldn't you say?

There is a way to make it more likely that you will recognise the partner that is truly right for you. This down-to-earth approach takes little away from the romance of a love affair except the rose-tinted spectacles. I want to show you how to learn to *like* as well as to love the person with whom you want to share your life, so that you not only find but also keep the love of your life.

You may still be grappling with the idea that you couldn't possibly choose a potential life partner the way you choose a fridge – the thought itself is pure heresy! But you'd be wrong.

159

And, if you've already had more than one mistake behind you, you might now be ready to give this a try. There are two stages:

Stage 1. First, you need to sort out in your mind what's important to you in a long-term relationship, what your needs, your desires, preferences and values really are. This is an extremely important first step and a much better approach than deciding what irritates you about your partner as you go along and then breaking up because you conclude that you're incompatible after all. At least this way, you can avoid a lot of pain and disappointment – on both sides.

Stage 2. When you meet someone that takes your fancy, you're now able to discover if this person shares your fundamental values, attitudes and outlook on life. This is not as hard as you might think because you don't have to do this all at once. Take your time. Ask questions, listen very carefully and pay attention to see if their actions and their words are generally consistent. Do they practise what they preach? Only then will you be able to make sound decisions about your future together.

So, start with Stage 1. Take your time. It may take several sessions over a period of weeks and you must *keep notes*. This is important.

Use this opportunity to discover what you can tolerate and what you can't. For example, given that none of us is perfect, if a potential partner had a habit that you found irritating but also a quality that you absolutely treasured, would you be able to live with the irritating habit without nagging and criticising? We're back to the analogy of the music and the coughing.

One other point. We all change over a period of time and, while most of our attitudes and values are said, astonishingly, to be shaped by the time we're seven years old, we're continually exposed to many experiences that can cause us to question our beliefs and reassess the things we thought were important to us. That's why I strongly suggest that you review and update your notes at least once a year and most certainly after a major event, either a fabulous one or one that is deeply upsetting. Both kinds can shake us up enough to make a review useful.

Below is a list of questions you might like to ask yourself; they need reflection and there are no right or wrong answers. It's all a matter of degree. It's what makes us who we are. For example, on the matter of spending time together, it's not a question of all or nothing but of how much. You will also have to make choices, asking yourself, for example, 'How much more important to me is this instead of that?' rather than, 'Do I prefer this or that?' The idea is for you to discover your most comfortable balance rather than having all or nothing.

Communication

Personal preferences

So much has been said about the importance of communication in a relationship that one might easily forget that people have what we call in the trade a 'comfort zone'. This zone sets out the limits within which we feel comfortable.

How reserved or communicative are you? Do you want to share everything, do you feel the need for privacy or are you somewhere in between? If you're both very reserved then intimacy may not be top on your list of priorities but, if you're very different in this area, one of you is going to feel very lonely. If you're a fairly private person, are you prepared to learn to express your feelings? Being out of step on this matter is the number one complaint, especially, but not exclusively, for women.

For some people there's no such thing as too much communication, while for others there obviously is. Where do you fit in? Do you prefer a partner who always tells you everything they're feeling or would you prefer somebody who's more reserved? And how reserved is reserved? Do you want to take the time to listen to your partner's feelings and thoughts or does this idea turn you off?

Selective listening

Hearing only what you want to hear can also become a real source of problems. To what extent are you prepared to hear things that may make you feel uncomfortable, without becoming defensive or anxious and putting up barriers? One example might be things that show that your partner is scared and vulnerable, not always strong and in control.

Personal communicating style

Some people believe in complete honesty and directness. They don't beat around the bush and, for them, lying is the worst possible sin. Other people take a different view. They say that tact, sensitivity and never deliberately hurting their partner's feelings is more important, which is why they also believe that the odd white lie here and there is perfectly acceptable. It's important for you to understand your own personal style, so ask yourself, which of the two is true for you, and to what extent? Think of examples to help you clarify your feelings.

Personal habits

Are there habits that you can tolerate and others you are not prepared to accept? Are any of these habits a matter of degree or not? Under this heading you may consider things like smoking, gambling and drinking. Are there any others that you need to think about?

Lifestyle

How important to you is a partner with status, a prestigious job, good promotion opportunities and a high salary? How important to you is your own career? How much time and energy are you prepared to devote to achieve it? What are you willing to give up for it? Does it matter who earns more? If your career is very important to you, you may experience conflict if your partner wants to invest more time in the relationship than you do. This can become a problem if one partner feels neglected.

How would you feel about your partner if they were to lose their job or business? How do you feel about role-reversal?

Money

Money tends to be one of the main sources of conflict in a long-term relationship. That's why you need to be absolutely clear about your attitude to it, what it means to you, and how you like to spend it. Also, ask yourself, to what extent do you expect to consult your partner or expect your partner to consult you when it comes to spending money? And what is your attitude to saving? Do you go out spending money if you're bored, frustrated or upset? Are you a spend-aholic? Are you a compulsive saver? Are you somewhere in between? You had better choose a kindred soul or sparks will definitely fly!

Involvement in each other's life

Would you like to devote your energies to support your partner in their work or do you prefer to concentrate on your own career, maintaining your own individuality? This need not be 'either or' but 'how much'. If you choose a partner in the same field as your own, what are the chances of you becoming more competitive? What would happen if either one of you became more successful than the other, for example, getting more promotions or earning more? How would you feel, and how would you handle it if either one of you is required to move to another part of the country for a promotion or greater career opportunities? If you both have careers and one of you had to stay put, how would you handle the separation?

Speaking of his ex-girlfriend Michelle Pfeiffer, Fisher Stevens said, 'There were tensions. It was a long-distance courtship and our relationship just couldn't take it.'

Physical affection

Are you physically affectionate or are you uncomfortable with displays of affection, either in private or in public? Some people hate to be touched, others feel distressed without frequent loving gestures such as hugging, stroking, kissing, or a simple peck on the cheek.

Do you tell your partner you love them? How much do you yourself need to hear it? Differences in this area can cause a lot of distress but relationships where both partners show and express their affection for each other are long-lasting, happy and fulfilled.

Children

Do you want children? When? How many? Women, do you want to stop working when they come or do you plan to become a working mother? What kind of support do you expect from your partner? Do you have any strong beliefs about how children should be raised? Do you have any strong feelings about how much time both of you should spend with the children?

In terms of general priorities, will your children come before your relationship or will your relationship come before your children? Is there any chance of either of you feeling jealous or left out, especially if there are stepchildren involved? Bad relationships with stepchildren are a major cause of breakdown in second marriages.

How would you feel if you – or your partner – couldn't have children? What alternatives would you be prepared to consider? What alternatives would you refuse to consider?

How would you feel if you – or your partner – didn't want to have children? Women, if you accidentally got pregnant, would an abortion be an option for you? And, if you did decide to have an abortion, what if your partner was strictly against it? You could end up having an unwanted baby on your own.

These are enormously important topics that you need to discuss in advance because afterwards it's too late. Don't expect your partner to change their mind after you're married. Remember: The seeds of divorce are planted in the early days of courting.

Expressing your appreciation for your partner

Do you tell your partner how much you appreciate them or do you believe that some things should be taken for granted? Do you operate on a 'no news is good news' way of managing your relationship? If you do, be warned: Lack of appreciation is complaint number two for both men and women.

Sex

What are your sexual expectations in terms of interest in sex, frequency of love-making, and actually initiating it? Big differences in this area can make you both unhappy.

Mimi Rogers, the ex-wife of Tom Cruise, complained that the reason for the breakdown of their marriage was that sex was much more important to her than it was to him. The difference was so strong that 'It became obvious that we had to split.'

Fidelity

How important is faithfulness to you? Don't make the mistake of taking anything for granted. If this is important to you – and it should be – then make it absolutely clear that this is one of your rules (see Chapter 7, Love: An Insider's Guide).

Sylvester Stallone is supposed to have said of his ex-wife Bridgit Nielson 'I couldn't take the fact that she was having affairs.'

Religion

Do you have any strong religious beliefs, is religion irrelevant in your life, or are you somewhere in between? How do these beliefs influence your life, your values and expectations? To many people's surprise, religion suddenly becomes important when children arrive.

Family and friends

How much time do you want to spend with family and friends? This may be an issue if, for example, one of you is an only child and the other comes from a large, noisy, gregarious family. How big a role do you expect your families to play in your relationship, how often do you expect to visit each other, when, for how long and how will you balance your obligations to both your families?

What are your expectations in terms of taking sides? About what issues? Could there be a problem with loyalty? Friction with in-laws is a well-known source of disruption and even separation. Remember also that one reason for relationship break-up is disapproval from family or friends.

Leisure

How much time do you want to devote to hobbies, sports and social activities? Do you prefer to do these things alone, with friends, with your partner or a combination of all three?

General considerations

There are two very important things that you may need to consider if they apply to you:

- Falling in love with someone from a different ethnic group, nationality or religion could create real difficulties in the long term. For example, some cultures have customs and attitudes you might find very difficult to live with, however much you love your partner.

- If your educational and social background is very different, you may end up feeling ashamed of your partner or you might have a crisis of confidence. This point and the previous one could also affect your relationships with family and friends.

I don't mean to imply that couples with different ethnic, social, religious or educational backgrounds cannot make it work, but if you're incompatible in very important areas you need to face the issues. Contrary to what we would dearly like to believe, love does *not* conquer all. You must not assume that it will 'be all right on the night'. Do discuss it.

The right partner for you is somebody with whom you're compatible and who shares a similar view of the world. The problem is that when we meet someone who really takes our fancy we want to show ourselves at our best. That's understandable but don't overdo it. Don't hide your opinions just because they're different from those of the other person. This would be a major mistake because if the relationship does progress you will both have to show yourselves as you really are. If you've been putting on an act, then your partner may experience a shock horror disappointment and a sense of having been cheated. Besides, the whole foundation would be flimsy and you can't grow a solid relationship on a flimsy foundation.

If you choose someone with whom you have a good match, you will make it far more likely that the two of you will grow together and change in a similar direction over the life of a long, happy and fulfilling relationship rather than, as so often happens, growing apart. And the reason this approach works is because people rarely change dramatically in their basic beliefs about the meaning of life, the universe and everything.

You should both be willing and able to adjust to some things but, in the more fundamental aspects, don't expect your partner to change, and I certainly wouldn't recommend that you compromise yourself because you will resent your partner in the long term. Ways people in love compromise themselves include giving up their friends, even their families; spending evenings in the pub when they don't like drinking; giving up squash or going to the gym; pretending they don't like classical music because their partner teases them about being 'toffee-nosed'; giving up their careers (especially women. Yes, even in this day and age! Big mistake!), and so on. Sooner or later, these things will end up causing a lot of resentment, so I urge you, please, please be true to yourself.

Let me tell you about Brigitte. Brigitte was over the moon and couldn't wait to tell me about this very special man she'd met about eight months ago. She's a lovely woman and tends to think that everybody is wonderful but – and this is a big but – she's not naive. This means that she's also observant. She started telling me about *him* and I'm going to highlight the important clues in her story that make me certain that this relationship has a good chance to work really well.

Brigitte explained that she'd met Greg at her Business in the Community project and then continued: '. . . So we got talking – and discovered that we had *all sorts of things in common*. Talking with him was easy. I noticed right away not only that he talked about things, but also *how he felt* about them, which I thought was *very appealing*. It also made it easier for me to get to know him and learn to understand what was important to him. That was very useful, because I discovered that *his outlook on life* is quite similar to mine.

'He's divorced and, in telling me about it, he only talked about how he'd felt in the relationship and what had prompted him to leave after so many years. But what I really liked about him, was that he *never overdid the criticism and the bitterness*. In fact, he's generally a *very positive person, like me*.

'Also, thank goodness, he's not a smoker. *You know how I absolutely hate smoking*, so once I became really interested in

him, that was a major relief. I don't know what I would have
done if he'd been a smoker.

'The other thing I noticed was that he's not a workaholic.
Although he has a good job he also likes to have a good time
and *we both enjoy* going to nice restaurants, the cinema and
the theatre. Unfortunately, he's not too keen on concerts but
that's OK, you and I can still go together so *it doesn't matter if
we can't do absolutely everything together*. Actually, *I prefer it
that way*. Anyway, he likes sailing – which does leave me cold.

'But the thing I really love about him is that he *truly listens to
me* and you know *how much I value that*. For me that's *pure
magic*. And, what's so wonderful is that *he's so encouraging
and supportive* and what's even more stunning is that he's *still
just as attentive*, just as *interested in my things, just as
supportive of my ideas* and *just as much fun to be with* as he
was at the very beginning.

'Not that long ago I went with him to visit a friend of his
family, and *I noticed how he treated her*. He was funny and
teasing but also took time to listen to her little stories, and was
generally very kind. Pretty much the way he's been with me all
these months. *It's the consistency*, you see. He's not just putting
it on to impress me. I also remember another occasion, where I
was talking over with him a problem I had with a colleague. A
client had given me some feedback about her and I was worried
about how to handle it. He told me that, whatever I did, I owed
it to her to talk to her face-to-face. That also told me that he's *a
basically decent person* who's *likely* to be straight with people
and *not likely* to cop out of difficult situations.

'And I'll tell you something else. He's so *affectionate*! He
likes to cuddle, and hold my hand or give me a peck. And his
back rubs! Well! But seriously, *that's really important to me*; it
may sound silly to you, but *it does make me feel loved*!

'In fact, I feel like he's also *my best friend*. And in the eight
months or so that I've known him, I've seen him in some of his
'off' moods too, so I'm certain that he's kind, loving and

thoughtful, and that we both have a good chance of making this work. I think this is *the real thing*, what do you think?' I thought she'd probably read this chapter . . .

If you read this story again you will notice that it's a bit like putting together a jigsaw puzzle. Things happen, circumstances change and there's a lot we can't even begin to know about a fellow human being but, if you pay attention, the pieces begin to fit together and you get an idea of how they're likely to act in the future.

TIPS

- Invest some time reflecting about what's important to you.
- If you're interested in a long-term relationship, then try to go for people with whom you have a number of values, opinions, interests and ideas in common. A compatible outlook on life will give you a better chance in the longer term.
- Even if you differ in some fairly fundamental areas, this doesn't mean that you have no future together. What it does mean is that you need to talk about these matters frankly and openly.
- Find out things about the other person by observing how they act, both towards yourself and towards other people, by asking them questions and by paying close attention to the answers. The key is consistency.
- Don't expect your partner to change.
- Don't compromise your basic values or beliefs. That would be the biggest mistake you could possibly make.

CHAPTER 18

What Do You Say After You Say 'Hello'? — How to Make a Genuine Connection

When we start talking with somebody new, we generally tend to keep to fairly safe and superficial topics. It's called chit chat or small talk and is very important because it's an easy way to decide whether or not we want to continue talking with this person or whether we would prefer to go back to mingling and try our luck elsewhere.

When we notice someone we're attracted to, we form a series of impressions. Once we start talking with them, these first impressions are either confirmed, added to or revised, because it's during this stage that we check each other out. Are they as interesting as they seemed to be from a distance? Do they appear to be interested in us? Do we have anything in common? At this stage, if you feel that you just don't click and that you don't really want to pursue this any further, you can withdraw very easily — without any permanent damage having been done to either of you.

As a rule, we like to be with people with whom we feel comfortable, so the point of small talk is to find out what, if anything, we may have in common, and how many ideas, interests, values and opinions we share — and the more, the better. Research by social scientists clearly confirms that 'Birds of a feather *do* flock together'. (This doesn't apply when lust strikes us like a flash of lightning, but many people have found out to their cost that, once lust has abated, they often have little, if anything, in common to keep them together.) Try to find out before you let yourself fall in love (yes, it is possible!).

Even – or especially – when you meet someone that takes your fancy, make sure not to look for their approval. Show yourself as you really are, express your true views and opinions and don't be afraid to disagree without attacking the opinions of the other person. If you try to impress them in order not to break the spell you will get yourself into real trouble. It might not happen straight away but soon – and just when that person was becoming really important to you.

You need to talk honestly and openly about yourself and who you really are. This is called 'disclosing', and it's the only way you can get emotionally close to another person and develop real intimacy. The most satisfying relationships are intimate ones because that's when we're known and accepted as we truly are, warts and all. When we learn to trust somebody, when we are comfortable being with them without feeling anxious and without the need to pretend, that's when we drop our defences and let love in. There's no other way and, yes, I know it can be scary. But it becomes less scary when you take it slowly, step by step, a little at a time. Intimacy is not instant. In fact, it's a little like a dance: I tell you a little about myself, you tell me a little about yourself, not too much at first. Then I tell you a little more and you do the same.

Disclosing is an art. If the other person starts telling you a lot about themselves but you're not responding, then they're likely to see you as cold, distant and stand-offish. If you tell them a lot of personal things and they're not responding in the same way, then they're likely to see you as overly familiar. Either way, you may both feel uncomfortable. Going *too fast, too soon* is one problem. Another is *not matching* the other person's rate of disclosure.

Go through this sequence: First, tell them something about yourself and then follow that with a question. Both these skills are examined in more detail below. The third one, listening carefully, is so important that I'm devoting the whole of Chapter 19 to it. These three skills, disclosing things about ourselves, both facts and feelings, asking questions, and listening carefully, are particularly important because they're the ones that make it easier to communicate with each other, not only at the very beginning of a relationship but also for as long as it lasts. And they're also the ones that will help develop relationships that are close and affectionate.

I will now go on to examine in more detail how to disclose in a way that is comfortable to you both. The whole thing flows really well when you take it in turns, as in a game of tennis, talking about yourselves, asking each other questions, and carefully listening to the answers.

Disclosing involves revealing personal things about yourself, your thoughts, your feelings, your likes and dislikes, your hopes and dreams, your proud and not so proud moments, your worries and anxieties, your joys and your sorrows, your views and opinions, things that are important to you, the things you enjoy, the things you don't, and why. The list is virtually endless. But trusting people with personal information can be scary and needs to be done slowly and gradually, over a period of time. Try to imagine the process as peeling an onion, one layer at a time.

In the beginning, deciding what and how much to disclose can be a bit tricky. It's best to start with fairly superficial topics mixed in with one more personal piece of information. Mention a fact about yourself and add how you feel about it. It's the combination of fact and feeling that enables people to find out what makes you tick. Then ask them a question about themselves.

After that:

1. Match the other person's rate of disclosure
2. Continue for as long as you feel comfortable
3. Gradually, over time, move on to increasingly personal information.

The point about opening up to another person is that you don't have to do it all at once. Remember the onion. It takes time to become close to someone.

When you share your most intimate thoughts and feelings you're showing that you trust the person in whom you're confiding, and that's flattering because being trusted makes people feel special. If you disclose intimate things about yourself to virtual strangers you're being foolish on two counts. Firstly, it can cause you real embarrassment later on, unless the other person is a total stranger and you will never see each other again. Secondly, it can be difficult for the other person to handle because they may wonder why you're telling them such intimate things and what you expect from them in return.

To give you some guidelines, there are five levels of self-disclosure. Things we might confide to:

1. a virtual stranger
2. an acquaintance
3. an intimate friend
4. members of our family
5. our partner.

Levels 3 and 4 are sometimes interchangeable depending on the relationship you have with your family.

But what happens when you start disclosing and the other person doesn't respond? It's tempting to think that they're cold and withdrawn but research has shown that this difference in rate of disclosure may be because of different conversational styles. Some people need a little longer to feel comfortable enough to start talking about themselves and they may need a little help so, if they don't seem to respond to your disclosures, try following them with an open question about them, then comment on what they've said and add something of your own. If this does not work it would be a good idea to stop in order to create some emotional 'space'. If you are sensitive to the other person's reactions you are more likely to get it right.

Occasionally, you may meet someone to whom you are so strongly attracted that you feel as if you've known each other forever. The truth, however, is that you haven't and even in such a case, before you can become real friends, never mind lovers, you'll have to learn a lot about each other. You will have to find mutual areas of interest and concern, sometimes do things together, discover perhaps the hard way how much you can rely on them to be there for you, and how far you're prepared to put yourself out for them. It's a journey that can't and shouldn't be rushed. You don't get to know another person overnight, and you need to feel comfortable to show yourself, warts and all, and know that you will still be accepted. In the early days you're still on your best behaviour which is understandable, but you can't build your whole future on that.

As friendships and relationships develop we discover that we're prepared to entrust some people with some things and other people with others. Similarly, we will become closer to some people than to others and that's good because we all need to have a variety of people in our lives, ordinary friends, best friends, acquaintances, some more casual than others and, perhaps, that special person.

So far so good, I hear you say, but how does one start sharing personal information? What can we tell people about ourselves? We might start by talking about what we do for a living and what we like about it, what frustrates us and why. Or about our hobbies and interests, maybe where we're planning to go on holiday and what attracts us about that place. If you like music or books, you might like to talk about that, which ones you prefer and what appeals to you about them. At first, it's better not to overdo the negatives. Focusing mostly though not exclusively on the good things tells our listener that we're a positive person who enjoys life. These are the kind of people we're all drawn to.

When it comes to asking questions, you can, at the beginning of your conversation, start with something fairly basic and safe, such as where they come from, how they spend their time when they're not working, what interests or hobbies they have, how they got involved with that particular hobby, why they chose it in the first place, what work they do, do they like it and why, and so on.

The idea is to help you get started, not to fire questions at them. When the other person starts answering your questions and you theirs, you begin to exchange a lot of 'free information' which is what you volunteer over and above what is strictly necessary to answer the question. This kind of information is the material that makes the conversation flow smoothly.

Take care not to monopolise the conversation without giving the other person a chance to contribute. People get bored very quickly if they're not allowed to get a word in edgeways.

It's the combination of disclosing, asking questions and listening that helps us not only to discover what we might have in common, but also to develop closeness over a period of time. And, if we're really smart, we will continue to use these skills – not only with a potentially romantic relationship, but with our friendships as well.

TIPS
- Sharing your thoughts, feelings and opinions is the only way to get closer to people. However, it's usually best to do it gradually and over a period of time, like peeling an onion, a layer at a time.
- Listen out for and volunteer 'free information'. It will give you both something to hook into and will make your conversations flow more easily.

- Don't monopolise the conversation; 'air time' should be shared more or less evenly.
- Practice the three skills involved in developing closeness: disclose personal things about yourself – the facts and how you feel about them, your thoughts, your feelings, your worries and your joys; ask questions; and listen attentively. Do this with both new and existing relationships.

CHAPTER 19

Listening –
The Ultimate Aphrodisiac

We tend to be attracted to people who show that they like us; we feel valued when people give us their undivided attention, truly listening to what we have to say. So, listening is one of the most important ways in which we can show the other person that they matter, that we're really interested in them and care about them. Listening is an act of love that makes the other person feel truly important and special – and when you listen and look into that person's eyes, you can get a glimpse into their soul.

Unfortunately, really good listening is not one of our strengths, mostly because we've never been taught how. Many people confuse listening with hearing but they're worlds apart. Lots of things can get in the way of good listening, such as what's going on around us, whether we're feeling too hot or too cold, or in some other way uncomfortable, or whether we're worried about something. When we're talking with another person, we tune in and out, we miss bits without even realising it, we assume we know what they're going to say next, and we start planning what we will say the minute they shut up – none of which makes us good listeners. This is not meant to be a judgement; it's what happens when we don't know any better and my purpose in writing this chapter is to show you that there is another way, a way that is extraordinarily powerful.

Listening is a skill that can be learned. In fact, many businesses have now recognised how important listening skills

179

are and have introduced it into their training programmes in order to reduce mistakes, wasted time, duplicated effort, misunderstandings, resentment and loss of goodwill.

To listen really well, we first need to make a conscious decision to do so. You may be tempted to think that, if you use the right 'non-verbal' listening skills like smiling and nodding, the other person won't notice that you're not really 'there'. Don't believe that for a minute! They can tell you're putting it on just as clearly as if you had a label 'not at home' stuck on your forehead. Never bluff! If you're too busy to listen properly then postpone it; say something such as, 'I can't give you my undivided attention right now. Can it wait until this evening? Then I can listen to you properly.'

Listening can't be rushed, it's a contradiction in terms. And you certainly can't listen if you're busy, because you will be distracted. The other person can always tell, so save yourself the aggravation of having to pick up the pieces afterwards with abject apologies, flowers and dinner. If you can't pay attention properly, explain why and postpone it.

How to listen really well

We may occasionally find that someone's words don't quite match their body language. When that happens, we subconsciously – and quite rightly – tend to believe the non-verbal clues because they're much harder to control and, if we pay attention, they're not difficult to interpret correctly. For example, think back to a time when you greeted someone by asking them: 'How are you?' and they replied, without smiling, 'I'm fine', in a flat tone of voice and with their eyes fixed on the floor. Chances are you knew there was something wrong.

Being aware of the impact of non-verbal communication can save you from unintentionally upsetting people. For example, if you doodle while you listen, the speaker may believe that you're not interested, or that you're bored, even if you really are paying very close attention. That's because, without any indication from you, they can't tell what you're really thinking and feeling.

Star listeners do a number of things that fall under four main headings:

1. *Body language or non-verbal communication*

- They pay total attention to the other person, as if they were the most important one around – which, of course, they are. They convey that interest by sitting or standing erect which makes their interest clear to the speaker.
- They never look over the speaker's shoulder to see what else is going on.
- They lean their head slightly forward towards the speaker, which indicates that they're concentrating on what the other person is saying.
- They spend quite a bit of the time looking at them.
- They nod occasionally, which encourages the other person to continue talking.
- They smile or use the facial expression that fits in best with what the other person is saying, which makes them look relaxed.
- They make supportive noises such as 'Uhu', 'Mmm', 'Go on . . .', 'Really!?', which tells the speaker that the listener is reacting to what they're saying.

2. *Verbal skills*

- They encourage the speaker by asking questions to help them clarify and expand on what they're saying. For example, 'Why did you think that?', 'What did you do then?', 'What happened?', 'What did she say to that?', and so on.
- They make sure that they understand correctly by summing up every once in a while, paraphrasing what the speaker said. This is particularly important when the topic is very sensitive, the person is upset, or the subject is complex or confusing. This is called 'reflecting back', and it is like holding up a mirror so the

person can see what you see – or hear what you hear.

A useful way to do this is to say something such as, 'So, what you're saying is that . . .,' as in 'What you're saying is that you got upset because he started shouting and you had no idea why', or '. . . you were pleased because he remembered without you having to remind him', or '. . . you're not sure how your boss will react to the news', or 'You must have felt great when it actually worked out as you hoped'.

This may seem a little awkward at first, but it's a very useful thing to do for a number of reasons. Firstly, it helps you understand more clearly and to sort things out if you misunderstood something; secondly, it shows the other person that you're really listening and trying to understand; and thirdly, it helps the speaker because, if they're feeling a little confused themselves, then 'reflecting back' can help them clarify their own thinking.

3. Reading the speaker's 'non-verbals'
They pay attention to:

- the expression in the speaker's eyes and face
- their gestures and mannerisms
- how they hold their body, for example, slumped or straight, turned towards or away from the person doing the listening
- whether their mood seems to be in tune with what they're saying.

Sometimes people will try to hide their feelings but, because you're now such a sensitive listener, you will work out their true feelings from their non-verbal clues. People will think you're amazingly perceptive – and, of course, they will be right!

4. Empathetic listening
This element is probably the most powerful of the lot because it focuses on you, the listener, trying to put yourself in the other

person's shoes, without judging or giving advice, unless they ask for it. The reason this kind of listening has such a tremendous impact is because it shows the other person that you respect them and that makes them feel accepted. Accepting that someone has a right to their opinions does not mean that you have to agree with them, but it recognises that, given their background, their experiences and their memories, it's not surprising that they feel the way they do and, if you were in their shoes, you would probably feel the same.

If you are thinking that the whole thing sounds just too, too complicated and quite hard work, and feel tempted to forget the whole idea, stop and think back to the last time somebody really listened to you, encouraging you to continue, obviously 'with you' and interested in what you were saying. Do you remember how you felt? Didn't you feel as if you were the most important person in the whole wide world?

On a slightly more light-hearted note, this kind of listening should really carry a red-light-for-danger sign because it's the kind that often makes people fall in love. It is no joke, though. When a sample of women were asked why they had affairs or left their marriages the reason most often given was that they had met somebody who truly listened to them and understood them. It made them feel visible and important again. So men, there you have it. And that goes for you women as well.

Something else that makes good listeners attractive and popular is that they come across as genuine people. There are two reasons for this. The first is that, when they listen, they don't censor, edit or put up defensive barriers; and the second is that they tend to reveal their own feelings, accept those of the other person and, best of all, they don't judge. No wonder they're so great to have around! Nothing makes us feel more valued, more important, and more cared for than this kind of listening.

Good listeners resist the temptation to interrupt – and they are not afraid of silence. You may be surprised at this, but silence tends to make most people anxious. They feel the need to rush in and fill it. And yet, silence can be extraordinarily powerful.

Poor listening can sometimes happen out of over-enthusiasm. Here's a true story about how good intentions can backfire. Many years ago, a friend of mine, Cris, came to see me. He started to talk about something and I got so involved with his story that I was not just with him, I was ahead of him. So I started interrupting and finishing his sentences. Honestly, there was no disrespect intended, it was just my way of showing that I was with him. It didn't work. He kindly tolerated it for a while until eventually, quite exasperated, he turned to me and burst out: 'Shut up damn you!' Well, that certainly did manage to shut me up! And it got me thinking. How many other friends had I unintentionally diminished by interrupting?

Recently, my hard work – believe me, it really is hard work, and I'm still working at it – to become a better listener was rewarded. Over the years, Cris and I had lost touch. No, it wasn't because of my constant interruptions – at least, I don't think so! Anyway, we recently and quite by chance met up again and, as you can imagine, we had a lot of catching up to do. As he started telling me things, he would occasionally fall silent. I said nothing. He started up again. Then he looked at me and said, 'You know, what you just did, giving me the space to clear my thoughts, made me feel really valued.' That's when I felt I'd arrived . . . Thanks, Cris!

Let me end with an 'inside tip': if you're wondering how you can tell when to stay silent, watch the eyes. When the speaker is thinking, they look into the middle distance and have that 'far away' look in their eyes.

REALLY TERRIFIC LISTENERS ARE PEOPLE WHO LISTEN
WITH THEIR EARS, THEIR EYES AND THEIR HEARTS

TIPS

- When you're with someone, give them your undivided attention, and put all your energies into listening and trying to understand them.
- If you're too busy to listen properly, say so and arrange a better time.
- Practise the listening skills described in this chapter.
- Watch the eyes. They tell you when to stay silent because they need to gather their thoughts.

CHAPTER 20

In Praise of Praise

You won't be too surprised to hear that, in a study about what people valued most in a close relationship, researchers at Yale University discovered that the top two groupings were 'communication' and 'support' followed by 'understanding' and 'appreciation'. Exactly what people have been saying at my workshops.

Earlier on I talked about letting people know that you like them. In this chapter I want to look at the role and impact of criticism and praise (or 'cold pricklies' versus 'warm fuzzies' which, I think, describes the feeling at the receiving end very vividly).

The bad news about criticism

First the bad news: criticism does not work. Yes, I know what you're thinking, 'If you don't tell people what they do that upsets you, how can they change?' That's a fair point and I will come back to it a little later.

Before that, let's talk about something else. How do we respond when people do things to please us? Do we acknowledge their efforts, praise them, compliment them, show them how much we appreciate what they did? No. We act as if it was only to be expected. We tend to treat our family, friends and neighbours, subordinates, colleagues, and managers, and, particularly, our partner or lover on a 'no news is good news' basis. But the minute they put one foot wrong, we don't waste a single moment in making our feelings known loud and clear. The downside is that, if we ignore these friendly and loving gestures, the people around us will soon get discouraged and stop doing them. One day we will wake up and realise that they're not happening any more, and then we will complain that nobody ever does anything nice for us. So, they're damned if they do, and they're damned if they don't. I call it setting them up.

There are two reasons why ignoring the good stuff and just criticising when people don't meet our expectations simply doesn't work. The first reason is that it promotes a negative environment that breeds resentment, and the second one is because, when a person is criticised, their first reaction is to justify and defend themselves, blame you, blame others, blame circumstances beyond their control, even blame the weather. The one thing they're highly unlikely to do is to accept the blame. Not only that, they will try to turn the tables on you, saying that you're always bitching, nagging, complaining, and that nothing they do is ever right. Someone will rarely say, 'You're right, dear, I screwed up.' In fact, I can think of very few situations that might force those words through a person's gritted teeth. Examples might include cases where the 'sin' is so major and the evidence so conclusive that there is no way of wriggling out of it; or if a person's sense of self-esteem is amazingly strong; or if they were to feel totally safe in their relationship. Then, and only then, might someone – perhaps, and then only reluctantly – admit they were wrong. So we must stop expecting it or, worse, demanding it from our partner.

Something which could save your relationship a whole lot of wear and tear is 'attribution theory'. Attribution theory is one of the techniques psychotherapists use to help couples change the way they deal with each other, by looking at how they interpret each other's behaviour. This is very important because we treat people according to how we interpret their motives towards us, either positively or negatively.

Let me give you two examples:

EXAMPLE 1

If you think your partner did something nice because they love you and wanted to please you, you will be thrilled, and perhaps hug and kiss them. But, if you think they did it just because they felt guilty about something, then you're likely to dismiss their kind gesture, treat them with suspicion, maybe acting frosty and saying something sarcastic.

EXAMPLE 2

Your partner arrives home late. If you assume they're selfish and thoughtless because they should have called you and didn't, showed no consideration for your feelings and how worried you've been, then chances are that, the minute they show their face through the door, you'll come down on them like a ton of bricks. If, on the other hand, you think that your poor mate was probably caught in a traffic jam – God knows there are plenty of those around – and that they're likely to arrive home frustrated, tired and ratty, then you're likely to welcome them more sympathetically.

The reason psychotherapists regard attribution theory as such an important and powerful tool in helping couples become aware of how they interpret their partner's behaviour is because it can become a self-fulfilling prophecy, confirming either your best or your worst assumptions about your partner. Depending upon which you choose, you will feel more or less loved and react accordingly – and so will they.

The more negative thoughts you think about your partner, the more you're likely to develop negative feelings towards them. That, in turn, will lead you to behave negatively, such as talking to them in a sarcastic tone of voice, acting in an aggressive, angry and disapproving manner, nagging, criticising and putting them down – or coldly ignoring them.

But, of course, there's the other side of the coin. The more positive thoughts you have about your partner, the more affection you will develop for them and that will encourage you to be more patient and tolerant, regarding any bad behaviour as a temporary aberration which is totally out of character (in the first example it's the kind behaviour which is regarded as totally out of character). You will be more inclined to do little thoughtful things for them to make them feel better – after all, it's just a temporary bad mood.

Sally, who attended one of my workshops, came to see me after I had spoken about how to become aware of the positive qualities of family and friends (Chapter 1). Obviously frustrated, she started telling me about her teenage son, how he couldn't do anything right, how he made a mess of everything, his room was like a bombsite, he looked really awful with that shaven head of his, his homework was a disgrace, how ashamed she was feeling in front of the neighbours, and so on. Then she said, 'I don't know how to do this exercise. There's nothing positive about him at all!'

I'm sure I don't have to draw you a map. This is the end result of years of nagging and criticising. The person at the receiving end feels about as tall as a worm and will try to get back at you in all sorts of ways which will in turn just prove your point (self-fulfilling prophecy). Their self-esteem and confidence is non-existent because they see themselves through your cold, critical and loveless eyes. You wonder, where has that loving person you used to care for gone? You certainly don't recognise what's in front of you. And so it goes on.

Sally and I had a long chat. Yes, it was hard; yes, the good bits were buried so deep inside her son that I bet not even he himself knew there were any, never mind Sally! And yes, she had to try. She had no choice. Not just because she needed to rescue her relationship with her son but also because, if she didn't try, he would grow up hearing his mother's critical voice. And we all know what critical voices can do to us.

You had better face reality: criticism is the fastest way I know to create resentment and destroy relationships. If you think I exaggerate, just remind yourself of what it feels like to

In Praise of Praise

be at the receiving end of it. The only effect criticism has is that it undermines our self-esteem and sense of self-worth; we like to think of ourselves as 'OK-people', so we find it really hard to see ourselves through eyes that are critical, cold and disapproving.

At the end of Anne Tyler's novel *Dinner at the Homesick Restaurant*, an old man, Beck Tull, tells his adult son why he walked out on his wife (and children) years before. 'She wore me out' . . . 'Oh, at the start,' Beck said, 'she thought I was wonderful. You ought to have seen her face when I walked into the room . . . When your mother and I were first married, everything was perfect. It seemed I could do no wrong. Then, bit by bit, I guess she saw my faults. She saw that I was away from home too much and not enough support to her, didn't get ahead in my work, put on weight, drank too much, talked wrong, ate wrong, dressed wrong, drove a car wrong.' This passage gives a sense of the cumulative effect of mounting criticism. Beck married his wife because she thought he was wonderful and that made him feel wonderful too. But then she stopped seeing the wonderful side of him, the side that had made her love him in the first place, and started to see only his flaws. It was seeing himself through her cold and critical eyes that made him feel awful – and that finally drove him away.

We all agree that 'nobody is perfect and that, after all, we're only human' but I don't think most of us really understand what these words mean. The point is not that they can help us justify our own imperfections with a shrug; they're meant to help us to be more tolerant, understanding and compassionate when other people turn out to be less than perfect. We all need some 'Brownie points' for at least trying to improve; otherwise we get discouraged and stop trying, and that would be a shame because trying and failing is part of learning.

There's a world of difference between constant fault-finding (or being showered with 'cold pricklies' all the time) and constructive criticism. The first one just wears people down,

191

while the second can be a helpful way of improving someone's behaviour. In fact, constructive criticism can be a good way of developing a close relationship, because it can help us learn to adapt to each other.

If Sally's story rang any bells for you, and you're keen to give the 'positive focus' idea which I described in Chapter 1 a try, start noticing the good things, and praise and compliment the other person's efforts and successes. However, be warned. They may not, at first, react in a particularly friendly or grateful way. They probably wonder what on earth is going on, are you after something or just being sarcastic. Don't be too surprised if that happens, and don't be too disappointed either. It's only to be expected. After all, if it was you, how would you react at the sudden change? Be patient.

How to give constructive criticism

Giving constructive criticism is an art. First of all, it's a waste of time to carry on about trivial things. How can you tell if something is trivial or not? If it's a matter of preference – you'd rather they did 'X' or that they didn't do 'Y' but you could live with it, if you really had to – then let it go. Stick to what matters, remember that nobody is perfect, and choose the right time to talk about it. (Bed is out!) Then think about why you want to tell them. Do you want them to do something differently, or do you just want to let off steam?

Once you know what you want, work out the best way to say what needs to be said. 'You're a selfish dog, leaving your dirty socks all over the bathroom floor! Who do you think I am? Your mother?' is probably not the best approach. Stating calmly that you'd appreciate it if he put his dirty socks in the laundry basket might get you better results, even if you have to repeat it several times. After all, changes don't happen overnight.

If you are upset by something your partner did – or something he did not do – experiment with different ways of trying to encourage them to change so you can get out of the nagging-sulking-rowing cycle. Try something along the lines of 'Please let's talk. I feel upset when you watch too much telly because I feel I don't get enough time with you', or 'I feel angry when your clothes fall all over the floor because I have to pick them up. Would you pick them up or at least drop them in one place?'

The idea is to specify *exactly* what upsets you, suggest a solution and then ask for their suggestions about making things work better. All this may sound complicated at first, especially if you're used to jumping in with both feet but, as I'm sure you know, this doesn't get you the results that you want. In any case, if you persist, after a while it will become second nature. The effort is definitely worth it. By the way, don't expect that, just because you said it once, you won't have to repeat it again and again. People seldom change immediately just because you've asked them to – you don't and neither does anyone else. So don't get ratty or sarcastic or impatient.

How to revitalise your relationship

If you admit that you have become or are in danger of becoming blind, deaf and generally lazy in your relationships with anyone who's important to you, then go back to the exercise in Chapter 1 where I asked you to focus on between three and five things you especially like, value and admire about everyone you know.

The reasons why compliments and praise work are not only because they help you stay aware of the other person but also because they help you to continue to see them as attractive and in a generally positive light. You must admit, both are excellent reasons for giving it a good try!

If you want fulfilling relationships, you have to make the effort to stay aware of the people in your life, focusing especially on the things you like about them. Do notice whenever people do nice things, either generally or for you in particular, the things that, more often than not, you tend to take for granted. This will give you the material you need for the next step, which is to take every possible opportunity to compliment and praise the people in your life. Research (yes, more!) has found that compliments and praise not only make people feel good about themselves but also encourage them to go on making the effort.

Evidence that the deepest need in human nature is the need to be appreciated is absolutely overwhelming. No one *ever* gets enough of it! If you doubt this, ask yourself: 'Do I get told that I am clever, capable, lovable, efficient and wonderful as often as I would like?' I bet your answer, as it almost always is in our workshops, is a definite 'No!'

Hand on heart, ask yourself, 'When was the last time I complimented or praised somebody?' At the workshops, the answers usually range from 'err . . .' to 'last week' and, although there are even some who say 'yesterday', they are in the minority. Did you notice how we see ourselves as paying people more compliments than we get? That could either be a fact, or simply the feeling that we're not getting as much recognition as we need.

Generally speaking, it appears that more women than men give compliments and praise, probably because they know how much they mean to people. Men, gestures of appreciation work wonders, so do make a conscious effort to give lots more to your partner, friends, family, people at work and new people in your lives. In short, to everybody. Women, the same applies to you!

The power of compliments

If you want your compliments and praise to work really well, you have to observe two important conditions. The first one is that you must never give praise with a sting in the tail. You know the kind of thing: 'That was a great report – shame about the spelling', or 'You look really great even if it did take you over two hours . . .' They're worse than nothing at all because they set the other person up. For a second they feel ten feet tall, only to come crashing down a moment later.

The other condition is never to expect anything in return. If you don't know what I mean, then think back. Can you remember a time when you paid someone a compliment and they reacted with 'What do you want?' Ask yourself if you only tend to compliment people when you want something. People resent that, because they know that you're only trying to butter them up to get your own way. If you want something from them, ask directly; if you want to compliment them, compliment them – but don't mix up the two.

The reason why people crave appreciation is because, although on the surface they may appear to be confident, self-assured and successful, that's not the way they see themselves. Most people believe that they're frauds and that, sooner or later, they will be found out. Though others may see them as having got their act together, deep down people need to be reassured, if only occasionally, that their efforts are being noticed and appreciated. That makes them feel they must be on the right track and encourages them to go on trying.

Complimenting people also has an unexpected spin-off. Apart from making people feel good and encouraging them to go on doing whatever it was you appreciated, there's a lot of evidence that shows that if you give people genuine compliments, they're more likely to see you as sympathetic, understanding, clearly a person of good judgement, and even attractive. So, when you begin to show your appreciation for others, you will find that people will start to seek you out. It all comes back to rewards.

To sum up then, giving 'warm fuzzies' and expressing our appreciation is a simple but really effective way of showing that we like, and are interested in, the other person. It also helps build warmth and closeness in all our relationships, romantic or otherwise, new and existing, close and casual.

But this way of being with people doesn't happen suddenly out of nowhere, especially since you can't know when you first meet someone who will become a good friend – or even the person with whom you will want to spend the rest of your life. And that's why I'm urging you to start now as you mean to go on. You set the tone. As with everything else in this book, you have to be the one to take the first step because, if you wait for the other person to make the first move, you could be in for a very long wait. Once you start, you must go on doing it, even if people don't respond immediately. Give it time to work, especially if you – or they – aren't used to it.

Why people find it hard to accept compliments and praise

It's all very well to encourage you to start giving compliments but that's not always as easy as it sounds. There are many people who sometimes find it difficult to accept them. How often have you complimented someone on something they did only to be told: 'It was nothing, any fool could have done it!' or, when you commented on how good they looked, they replied, 'What! My hair's all greasy! I haven't washed it in days!', or something equally absurd and tactless.

So what's the problem? The fact is that many of us are afraid that if we just accept the compliments people might think that we're big-headed. I also believe that there's another issue here and that's our secret fear that perhaps we are unworthy and don't really deserve them. There is a lot of 'inner noise' going on that literally prevents us from being able to accept a compliment. Take my friend Richard. He had been doing some work and had done a really great job, and I told him so. He replied, 'Yes, we all did.' I said, 'I didn't mean "you all", I meant you specifically.' He appeared very uncomfortable, then looked at me and said, 'I can see what I'm doing but I find it really hard to accept compliments.' Then he smiled and added, 'But I'm getting better, don't you think?' We go back a long time, Richard and I . . .

If you recognise this scenario, then there are two things you can do. You can start by letting people know, not just once or twice, but probably many times over, that it's OK to accept compliments. Tell them gently and with a smile, 'Just breathe in, listen to the compliment, let yourself enjoy it, and then shut up!' In some severe cases, you may need to tell them that their reaction is like throwing the compliment back in your face, making you feel as if you had bad judgement or poor taste, and that you don't like that. Chances are that they had no idea how their reactions would make you feel. They probably thought they were just being modest. That's how it was with Richard, but he's learning . . . Be patient with them and keep letting them know that they're OK.

If you're like one of the people I just described, then remember that accepting compliments gracefully has nothing to do with being big-headed. Do make an effort to learn to accept them because someone did take the trouble to notice, to come up to you and tell you, and it is quite disconcerting to have the compliment thrown back in one's face. So, when someone pays you a compliment, just smile and say, 'Thank you, I'm glad you like it.' Then bite your tongue and resist spoiling it. You may need to work at this, but work at this you must! One thing that will help you is strengthening your self-esteem, a subject I will be exploring in Chapter 24, How to Care for Yourself: The Magic of Self-esteem.

Here are a few examples of powerful compliments and praise that really work:

- 'Christine, your new haircut looks terrific! It really suits you! It highlights your cheekbones – you look really great!'
- 'Brian, I love the way you garnished this chicken dish – all those colours make it look so appealing! And it tastes as good as it looks!'

197

- 'Jo, this report is very well written. It's balanced, brief and to the point. Well done!'

Those compliments contain two essential elements:

1. They're prefaced with the person's name which makes the compliment more personal
2. They are specific.

It's really important that your praise be as specific as possible, because it tells people exactly what they did well, so they can go on doing it. If the compliment is too general, they may still enjoy hearing it but they won't be too sure what exactly it was that you liked. It may seem obvious to you, but not to them.

Also, timing is everything! Make sure you react as soon as possible after the event, so they can see the connection between your appreciation and their action. That's an important part of what is called in the jargon 'reinforcing the behaviour' (a horrible if accurate term). The same applies to constructive criticism. Mention it as soon as possible along the lines explained earlier. A technique business trainers use is called 'behaviour modification', which encourages change by rewarding changes in the desired direction, rather than punishing disappointing behaviour.

Here are a few suggestions of things you can compliment people on.

- Something they've done
- Some special quality that they have, such as their cheerfulness; their enthusiasm; their optimism in the face of difficult times; the fact that you can count on them to keep their promises; their support when you need it; their broad shoulder and caring listening – the possibilities are endless. The compliment here is that you value the way that those qualities make you feel, rather than simply commenting on their nature

- The way they look, for example, something they're wearing
- Their taste, for example, the way they furnished their apartment, some particular ornament, or their choice of music.

And here's a really special tip, the one that's going to give a powerful edge to your compliments. When you compliment someone, choose an area that *they* value and find especially rewarding. We usually tend to comment on things that we would love to have for ourselves. For example, if we'd love to be fluent in other languages, we're more likely to admire and compliment people who have this talent, but this might not be particularly meaningful to them if they never had to work particularly hard at it. If something comes easily to someone, they tend to take it for granted. On the other hand, they're more likely to appreciate a compliment about something they feel unsure about or have had to work hard to achieve or overcome.

If you pay attention to the less obvious, you will make a major impact. There are two reasons why this works so well. First, it reassures the person that they're on the right track and making visible progress (or you wouldn't have noticed), and secondly, you will grow enormously in their estimation, because few people are perceptive enough to notice or to take the trouble to work out what the other person would truly value. That's because most people tend to focus on the obvious.

In Chapter 1, I suggested you picked two or three things you really like about everyone you come across and explained that the things that are likely to appeal to you about people will vary depending on whether you've only just met, whether you're on your way to getting to know each other better, or whether you know each other quite well.

In the beginning you, both men and women alike, will be attracted by a person's appearance, which includes the way they dress, their voice, the way they speak, and so on. You then might decide that you like their manner, their attitude to life, their friendliness, or some other pleasant quality. After that come features that you personally value and things they do that you appreciate and admire. Making it a point to be aware of these will give you plenty of material for compliments at various stages of your friendship and for as long as you stay together which, if you follow the suggestions in this book, will be a very long time.

In my workshop there is one session which has proved one of the most popular ones, where everyone has to give everyone else a 'warm fuzzy' (they do get advance warning). The only rule is that they're not allowed to return it. All they're allowed to do is to accept it, let it warm them (hence the term 'warm fuzzy'), and try to let themselves enjoy the feeling. The sight of people initially a little embarrassed, but at the same time loving it is really something to behold!

You can make this happen wherever you are. Don't you remember how wonderful you feel when someone takes the trouble to come up to you and compliment you about something, whatever it may be? People bask in the warmth of compliments and remember them long after you've forgotten all about it. So take the initiative and start spreading those warm feelings whenever you can!

TIPS

- Criticism, especially the fault-finding kind, is undermining and destructive. It's a bad habit that you need to unlearn – fast!
- People need 'Brownie points' to encourage them to keep on trying. Give them plenty.
- Thoughtful and caring criticism can bring people closer together. The art lies in deciding which are the important issues and in learning to live with the rest; thinking about why you want to tell them; choosing the right time; and then working out the best way to say it.

- For compliments to work they must never have a sting in the tail, and they have to be given without expecting anything in return.
- Good compliments are prefaced with the person's name and are specific.
- They're also given as soon as possible after the event so people can connect your praise with their action.
- If the other person has difficulty accepting a compliment, be patient with them but help them take it in and accept it. Don't let them brush it off.
- If you yourself have a hard time accepting compliments make an effort to learn to accept them. Protests make people feel rejected. Chapter 24 will help you build your self-esteem.
- You can compliment people on the way they look, on something they're wearing, something they have, something they did, or some personal quality that appeals to you. Use the material from the exercise in Chapter 1.
- Choose to compliment people in areas which they feel unsure about or which they're trying hard to improve. It will work wonders for their self-esteem and show you for the perceptive person you are.
- Take every possible opportunity to give compliments and praise.

CHAPTER 21

The Power of Touch

Talking about touch can be a bit like opening a can of worms, so much so that this topic used to be considered something of a taboo area. One only had to say the word and people would giggle or squirm with embarrassment because of the sexual connotations. This used to be a peculiarly British reaction as other cultures such as the Latin-American, Spanish, French, Italian, Arab and African are very comfortable with touch. For them talking and touching are closely intertwined. On the other hand, people from colder climates and cultures, such as the British, tend to feel uncomfortable with touch, and some regard it even as somewhat threatening. That can lead to difficulties and misunderstandings when people from different cultures meet, both in social and business contexts.

I was brought up in Argentina, and in an Italian neighbourhood to boot, so for me, touching and talking went hand in hand, like bacon and eggs. The idea that one could talk without touching never occurred to me. When I first came to England in 1965, I had some major adjustments to make. In fact, I would sometimes land myself in awkward situations, because men would think that I was giving them the come-on, while women appeared extremely uncomfortable. And neither knew what to make of me.

Things have changed dramatically, thank goodness! Nowadays, people are much more relaxed with touch and I have come up with two possible explanations that might account for this. One is that Britain has become a nation of peoples of all races, nationalities, cultures and religions and these days people travel a lot more both for business and pleasure so they've become more used to different cultures.

In addition, I've become more skilled at it. With some of my friends the type of touching we do is unique to that friendship because there's an additional cultural dimension involved. When my friend Paola and I meet, we hug in pure pleasure at seeing each other again. So far, this is nothing terribly special because I do this with my other friends too. But then, as we set off for lunch, she will tuck a hand under my arm (it's usually she who does it because I'm the taller one). I love that gesture because, apart from the obvious affection, it also brings back memories of Argentina where young girls used to walk around arm-in-arm. And I also recognise that, as an Italian, Paola's and my own social background are similar to one another's and it feels a little like 'home'.

If you are a woman, tucking your hand under a man's arm is a very seductive thing to do. Beware, though, because even if you didn't quite mean it that way, the man is very likely to interpret that as a flirting gesture.

To touch people appropriately so you can increase the chance of a positive reaction, you need to know the rules and develop the skills involved. We have all at one time or another come across people who make us feel uncomfortable when they behave in an overly familiar manner, yet touching has such a major impact on both our social, business and personal lives that we need to understand it a lot better and to learn to become really good at it. Once we understand the ins and outs of touch, we will feel less anxious about the whole thing. At the same time, learning the rules and the skills will show us an important way to influence our relationships for the better, because touch is communication at its best; it serves to underline the message and can also be used to express all kinds of non-sexual feelings and emotions.

The impact of touch

The topic of touch is extremely complex and there have been many books written about it (a very good one is *Touch Therapy* by Helen Colton) so I intend to keep it simple.

First of all, how, where and when you touch others can make or break your relationships. As long as you remain aware of the other person's reactions, if the intention and purpose are appropriate then most people, most of the time will react well to your touch. I'll go even further: in certain instances it may even be regarded as insensitive *not* to touch, for example, if someone were to burst into tears and you just stood there without even trying to comfort them by patting them on the hand or by putting a hand on their arm. But more of that later.

There are a number of very strict rules on the subject of touch, and rule number one is that you need to be sensitive to the other person's feelings and reactions at all times. As with all other areas of communication there are two points of view: yours and the other person's, and with touch, as with other types of communication, what really matters is not so much what you intended but how the other person interpreted it.

To start with focus on areas under your own control. There are a number of things you need to think about, the simplest of which is whether or not to touch in the first place. After that it gets a little more complicated. *When* is it OK to touch? *Where* is it OK to touch? *How* do I do it so I don't put the other person off?

Next, you need to learn to interpret their body language correctly. This is really not as hard as you might imagine and, once you've learned what to look out for, you'll be more sensitive to their needs and reactions and that, in turn, will help you to behave skilfully and appropriately.

Remember Chapter 19, Listening – The Ultimate Aphrodisiac where I described the clues that betray the other person's true feelings? Well, similar clues apply here as well. If, when you touch somebody, they feel uncomfortable, they're likely to pull back, stiffen, frown or generally look ill-at-ease, so pay attention to the expression in their eyes and face. They might even blush which could indicate embarrassment. Watch their posture and gestures. For example, when people feel ill-at-ease they tend to close in and tighten up their bodies, that is, they also look physically uncomfortable. If, on the other hand, they don't mind, they might remain relaxed, not react at all, or perhaps look comforted, smile or lean towards you.

The power of touch lies in the fact that its effect can be very subtle. I once read about an experiment in an American library which really makes the point. The librarian's job was to hand out and receive back books from customers. Her instructions were to say exactly the same thing to each person and to be sure not to smile. The only difference was that, in some cases, she would lightly brush her fingers against the customer's when the books changed hands while, in others, she took care not to touch them at all. The exchanges were observed by a researcher who would signal to another indicating 'this customer was touched' or 'that customer was not touched'. The customers were then interviewed and asked a number of questions about the quality of the library's service including whether or not the librarian had been friendly and approachable. The last question was 'Did the librarian smile?' And then, almost as an afterthought: 'Oh, by the way, did the librarian touch you?' Here are the results:

1. Those who had not been touched said the librarian had not smiled, and that the service was OK, nothing special
2. Those who had been touched said the librarian had smiled at them, and that the service had been really efficient and friendly

3. *But* nobody remembered being touched, even those who had been.

What the results showed was that the touch conveyed friendliness and warmth, irrespective of whether or not the person smiled even though smiling is the usual way we show that we're friendly people.

So what touch does is to give us an added way of connecting with people. In fact, it's a powerful way to nurture a relationship, to show that we care, and to break down barriers with even the stuffiest people.

How to interpret the meaning of touch

Imagine you're talking with someone. They're standing fairly close to you and they have touched you a couple of times. Rather than assuming immediately that the other person is overstepping the mark, ask yourself the following questions to help you interpret correctly what is happening:

- Is the room very crowded or is there a lot of space around you? Being in a crowded place is often one of the reasons people stand very close to each other.
- Is this a social or business situation?
- Are you both of the same or opposite sex?
- Are you both of the same or different nationalities or cultures?
- What is your relationship now and what would you like it to be? For example, is this a business relationship or are you both equally attracted to each other?
- What is the stage of the relationship? For example, you may both feel attracted to one another but have only just met so it may be a question of timing rather than of not liking that person.
- If this is a work situation, is one of you senior to the other?

- Are you aware of your individual differences, similarities and preferences as far as touch is concerned?

(For more on touch in the sexual context, please see Chapter 22, How to Develop a Fulfilling Sexual Relationship.)

Once you've interpreted the other person's behaviour, you will be able to make some decisions of your own. You may choose to accept what's happening or, if you feel uncomfortable, you might either say something such as, 'You're going a bit too fast for me' when you just want to slow things down a little, or 'Please don't touch me; it makes me feel uncomfortable' when you feel the other person is 'trespassing'. This way of expressing yourself is perfectly acceptable both in social and work situations.

Touch can be used as a way of exercising power, especially at work. Research into sexual harassment, which is the formal term for this kind of unwelcome attention, has shown that it isn't only men who do it; although it is much rarer, senior women have also been known to take liberties with subordinates. There's no need to suffer in silence because there is help available. There are courses on assertiveness and positive communications, and countless books on the subject which you can find in the Self Help section of all leading bookstores. You may also have a supportive colleague at work or you might be able to turn to your Personnel Department or Trade Union representative. Sexual harassment is against the law and is taken very seriously by employers. So please, whether you're a man or a woman, if someone behaves towards you in a way that makes you feel uncomfortable or upset, don't just clench your teeth and suffer in silence. Do something about it!

If you are dealing with people from different cultures, take that into account when trying to interpret the meaning of their touch because reacting too abruptly could cause offence and, in business, this could be bad news. Establishing rapport is often critical to closing a deal, so, if your job requires you to do a lot of travelling and to conduct business with people of other countries you may find it helpful to learn more about the do's and don'ts of different cultures. Contact some of the major business schools or the larger business reference libraries, which will be able to give you information on the range of cross-cultural courses available.

As mentioned in Chapter 10, What Attracts People to One Another?, 93 per cent of the impact we make on people comes before we even say a word, and touch and distance between people are two very important components of that impact. How we act ourselves and how we react to others will affect how people feel about us.

To sum up: to help you decide what is appropriate in the context of touch and space (the distance between people when they're talking or standing together) take into consideration the four main factors:

- The type of relationship you're engaged in
- The situation you are in, either social, business or private
- The culture of the people involved
- Personal preferences.

Please don't be scared off by the apparent complexity. All human beings have a deep need to be touched, and people who feel uncomfortable with physical affection often had little love shown to them when they were children. However, even they can learn to find comfort in being touched, if they let themselves, because touch supports, shows appreciation and affection, as well as demonstrating attraction.

Touching in loving relationships

One reason there's so little non-sexual touching in many love relationships is rooted in deep-seated anxieties and fears. Let me give an example. Many women still believe that, if they touch their partner, he will think that she wants sex when all she really wants is to show – and receive – affection. Men are also likely to have mixed feelings about purely non-sexual touching even though the '*Hite Report on Male Sexuality*' concluded that most men yearn for more tender and non-sex-related touching from women. It's so sad: both want the same thing from each other and neither knows exactly how to ask for it or even how to express it. Non-sexual touching in a loving relationship can make a partner feel loved and cherished. In a previous chapter I talked about the damage we can cause by taking our partner for granted and how, through lazy habits, we stop noticing them. Picture the following scenarios, in which I'll use typical role stereotypes because the behaviour is also generally typical of men and women.

SCENARIO 1

A woman has been home all day looking after a child, rushing around, trying to fit it all in. She's tired, frustrated, and longs for adult company and a little affection. Her partner comes home while she's in the kitchen preparing a meal. He shouts 'Darling, I'm home!' and, as she goes out to welcome him, he gives her a distracted peck on the cheek without even looking at her. He walks past her and flops in front of the telly. She's dying to talk about her day and hear about his. But there's nothing. How does she feel? Deprived? Lonely? Frustrated? Resentful? Taken for granted? All five and more?

SCENARIO 2

A man has been out all day working in a crowded office. His boss is on his back, people are complaining, phones are ringing, interruptions come from all sides, crises mount. And this is on a good day. She's got it easy, he thinks, all day in a lovely home with the baby. The weather is warm. He bets they're in the garden, relaxing. He'd change places with them any day. By the end of the day he's absolutely exhausted and he's had enough – except he still has the traffic jam to face. He arrives home and shouts 'Darling! I'm home!' She comes out and starts telling him about her day. He grunts something, gives her a peck on the cheek and escapes to the living room where he flops in front of the telly at last, dead beat. He hears her saying something but he can't be bothered to tune in. He dozes off . . . He's probably too tired to notice but his relationship is in trouble. Women say 'we don't talk any more', men say 'she keeps on at me. She says things like " let's talk" but talk about what?' One feels ignored while the other feels got at.

How to heal a relationship

You may think this is hopeless but, in fact, with a little bit of goodwill and very little effort, you can heal this relationship. And do you know how? Through non-sexual touching. You don't even have to say a word, at least not then. To those of you women who identify with the woman in my first scenario I'd say – timing is all. Dumping on him the minute he walks through the door is not a good strategy. He has nothing left to give. What he needs is about an hour or so to recharge his batteries. Men, if you can recognise yourself in my second story, there's something you can do to make your partner feel that she is, well, your partner and that you're both in this together. Look at her when you give her a peck, hold her a moment, touch her cheek, say something like 'It's so good to be home! I need to get myself together. Can we talk a bit later?'

But this isn't all by any means. Showing affection through non-sexual touching is something that you can do any time, even when you're busy with other things. Here are a few examples:

- As you pass each other put an affectionate hand across your partner's shoulder or give a quick teasing pat on the bum
- Take a second off whatever you're doing to place an open palm on your partner's cheek while looking them in the eye and smiling

- Touch their head fleetingly on your way to the kitchen
- Look at them and smile as you bring them a drink
- In the evening, nothing feels more wonderful than a neck and shoulder massage, a back rub or a foot massage.

I bet you can think up lots of other ways to make your partner feel noticed, visible, loved and cherished.

You may wonder, why is she talking about what happens in relationships if this book is about meeting new people? Good question. The answer is that you have to start as you mean to go on. Resentment in a relationship doesn't happen from one day to the next, it builds up slowly and insidiously over a period of time. If you dump on each other or take each other for granted when you're together, then the chances are that the seeds of this were planted early on in your relationship. An ounce of prevention is better than a pound of cure.

As I explained earlier, an important part of the skill of touch is being sensitive to the other person's reactions, especially with new people. There are some people who simply don't like to be touched, full stop, and you have to respect that so, if they look obviously uncomfortable, back off. Remember the clues? Stiffening, pulling the hand back, trying to shake your hand off or frowning are all indications to watch out for. If this happens, all you have to do is calmly remove your hand and lean back. You will now have restored space between the two of you which is obviously important to that person. If they either don't react to your touch or seem comforted, then you may leave your hand a moment longer before removing it, and you can remain leaning slightly towards them to show your continued interest. It is important to be sensitive to their feelings and needs rather than your own. If they don't appear to be grateful for your warm concern, don't think, 'Oh my God! I've just been rejected!' and retire sulking into a corner.

Touching is more than a simple expression of sympathy or

friendliness. It can become all important, for example, when words seem inadequate to express how you feel. And touch can, literally, be health giving. For example, touch is absolutely necessary for the survival of babies. Premature babies are hyper-reactive and must not be touched too much. However, twenty minutes of gentle, rhythmic stroking helps some of these babies to develop more quickly, leave hospital sooner, and become healthier and more alert than other premature babies. Even healthy babies, if deprived of touch for long periods, withdraw and become apathetic. In extreme cases, they may even wither away and die. Food and medical care by themselves are not enough to keep babies and young children alive.

Older people can suffer from 'touch-starvation' or 'skin-hunger' too, especially when their partners have died and their families and friends have moved away. It's the lack of touch and human contact that's the hardest thing to bear.

Research results into the power of touch are consistent: touch is a unique way to show interest, affection, appreciation, caring, understanding, compassion, enthusiasm, and many other positive feelings. And touch can even increase someone else's liking for you. This has to do with rewards, which I have already mentioned in the context of attracting and keeping people in relationships – both love and friendship. Your affectionate touch communicates your feelings to the other person; that, in turn, makes them feel good about being with you. They feel rewarded and feeling rewarded makes them like you more. Simple, isn't it?

The meaning of touch

The three things that give touch different meanings are:

A. the firmness of the touch
B. how long the touch lasts
C. which part of the body is touched.

There are five levels of touching:

1. The professional touch (doctor-patient, hairdresser, sales assistant when trying on clothes and shoes, tailor or dressmaker, chiropodist, masseur, etc.)
2. Touching between colleagues (shaking hands, a brief touch on the hand, arm or near the shoulder)
3. Touching between friends (hugging, putting an arm across the shoulder, clapping on the back and comfort handholding)
4. In family and in loving sexual and non-sexual relationships, (touching cheek with open palm, rubbing back, hugging, kissing, hand-holding, playing footsie)
5. Touching between lovers (as in point 4 plus sexual touching).

As I mentioned earlier on, there are people who, for whatever reason, dislike being touched. The worst of all possible worlds can come about in a love relationship where one partner needs demonstrations of physical affection and feels deprived and rejected without them, while the other feels stifled by attempts at physical closeness. I hope that, having spent time reflecting on what's important to you, you have been able to side-step this potential minefield and great source of misery. But, if I've come too late and you've already fallen in love with someone who is very different from you in this respect, slowly try to learn to meet your partner halfway.

If you're the one needing physical affection, take it easy and don't rush things. Slowly, gently and, above all sensitively, try to awaken your partner's positive feelings to being touched and help them learn to feel safer and more comfortable with it, little by little. It's like desensitising someone against a phobia and it can be done with a little goodwill on both sides. If you're the one who dislikes being touched, and you genuinely love your partner then try to meet them halfway when they express their need for physical affection. Lack of the occasional hug, peck on the cheek, warm squeeze on the arm, stroking of the cheek and so on can be immensely distressing and leave your partner feeling deprived and unloved.

In loving relationships touch plays a very important part and, as the relationship progresses towards greater intimacy, the types of touch the couple exchanges follow a specific sequence. For more on this, read Chapter 22.

Where to touch

The rules of touch are quite strict. There are specific areas of the body that are OK and some which are strictly 'no-go' areas. That applies just as much to relationships between men and women as to people of the same sex, especially in the case of friends or people we don't yet know very well.

Hands, forearms, upper arms and shoulders are 'accessible' areas, which means that they can be touched by anybody, men and women.

The head, neck, chest (especially women's), lower back, bottom, legs and thighs are 'off limits', which means they can only be touched by people in a professional context or by people with whom you are close and intimate.

What kinds of touch are there?

I've been using the very general term 'touching' but what do I mean by it? Touching is a social as well as a personal way of communicating and can include any number of different things ranging from formally shaking hands, to physically guiding someone across a street, towards a chair or through a door, one or two brief touches during a conversation all the way to more familiar and loving touches like hugging, stroking, hand-holding, intertwining fingers, and so on.

For example, when you're introduced to someone, the polite thing to do is to shake hands. The warmth of this touch can influence in a positive way how people feel about you as long as it is reinforced by the way you behave. If you shake someone's hand warmly, but then behave in a cold and distant fashion, without smiling or looking at them, the other person is likely to feel confused. On the other hand, holding someone's hand a shade too long if you've only just met, may be seen as embarrassing and too familiar.

In the beginning, if you want to progress towards a warmer, friendlier and more relaxed relationship with somebody, you can use a very casual kind of touch. For example, touching an arm to call attention to something or an 'accidental' nudge are both acceptable ways to move matters on to a closer footing.

How to get started

If you feel a bit unsure about how to start, then remember that your friends might quite like to be touched but might be equally confused. Throughout this book, I've been encouraging you to take the initiative, and I'm not about to change my tune now. You initiate touch. Chances are your friends will love it even if they're not one hundred per cent sure at first.

How often have you wanted to do something but weren't sure whether you should or not until someone 'gave permission' by doing it themselves? Then you feel it's OK to do it too. Permission can come from different sources: authoritative research, books or articles, as well as someone doing what you've been wanting to do all along. What I'd really love you to do is to become the one who gives others permission.

If you want to develop this particular skill, and I really hope you do, you might like to read about it first, and then go for it! But – and this is an important but – start by practising with 'safe' people like your family and friends, slowly moving on to people outside your close circle.

Here are some ideas you can try.

- When you're sitting talking with a friend, lightly touch him or her on the forearm, upper arm or shoulder at regular intervals. Don't make a big deal of it but do it when you want to underline something you're saying or to emphasise your reaction to something they've said.

- When a friend appears tired, comment on it with a soft, caring tone of voice and rub his or her upper shoulders, neck and back. *Don't ask first*, just do it. People who would really love you to do it are often likely to say 'no' if asked, just out of embarrassment.
- After a pleasant evening with a friend, put your hand briefly over his or hers. You could add something along the lines of how good you feel in his or her company, or how much you enjoyed the evening together.
- Touch a friend's cheek with an open palm in hello or goodbye while looking at them and smiling.
- Use the same warm gesture to say thank you. It can work wonders.

The magic of touch is that it often makes words unnecessary.

If you care for the other person as a human being and observe the tips given in this chapter, you should become really skilled – then watch how people warm to you!

TIPS
- Think of touch as touching the child that exists in every one of us who longs to be held and 'baby'ed'. Touch shows appreciation, it supports and comforts as well as indicating attraction.
- Don't forget that, in the hands of the unaware or insensitive, touch can be a double-edged sword. Do familiarise yourself with the *when*, *where*, and *how* of touch so you can learn to do it well.
- Be sensitive to the needs of the other person. Observe their physical reactions and respond accordingly.
- To interpret the meaning of touch, pay attention to the

circumstances, the type of relationship and the culture of the person involved.

- Because touch can make the other person feel good, it can increase their liking for you. It's all part of the rewards that keep people in relationships. Learn to use touch well; it will make your relationships much more fulfilling.

- If you're in love with a partner who is very different from you in terms of needing or disliking physical affection, then try to learn to move closer to each other. Otherwise, you will both be unhappy.

- Finally, read Helen Colton's *Touch Therapy*. It's very good indeed.

CHAPTER 22

How to Develop a Fulfilling Sexual Relationship

Recognising the person who's going to be a good partner for you is a big challenge. However, by now I expect that you will have given the matter quite a bit of thought with the help of the questions in Chapter 17, How to Recognise the Right Partner for You. One very important area is that of sexual compatibility – and by this I mean being more or less in synch with each other. But how can you tell? There's a growing move towards saving yourself for marriage and, given the high health and emotional risks of experimentation, that does sound very sensible. But, while I'm totally against experimentation, I don't believe that it's a good idea to wait until you're married to make love. You might then discover too late significant differences which could make you both unhappy – depending, of course, on how important sex is to both of you.

But let's go back to the beginning. Sexual attraction or passion can happen in one of two ways:

1. It hits us over the head like a flash of lightning
2. It grows as a result of gradually getting to know, like and love the other person.

Mistakes people make
While it's obviously not impossible for a solid relationship to

develop in the first case, the odds are against it, because sex tends to raise unrealistic expectations. The reason why instant sexual attraction is so risky is because it can make us believe that this is 'the real thing'. Many people, and not necessarily always women, mistakenly believe that, just because they've had sex, they're now in a real relationship, and they also often believe that because they've had sex, they're also intimate with that person. If you stop and think about this, it's not really all that surprising if you consider how physically intimate the sexual act is. In addition, either one of them may have said things such as 'I think I'm in love with you' to get the other person into bed. The truth is that, as we all know, sex can open up a whole can of worms.

On the other hand, if you're after a real relationship with this person, and you want to be as sure as possible (remember, though, that there are no guarantees), then making friends first, developing genuine closeness and intimacy, and learning to trust and understand each other is a much firmer basis for a fulfilling and lasting relationship. Another important mistake people often make is to think that friendship and passion are mutually exclusive. They couldn't be more wrong. In fact, having sex too soon can get in the way because afterwards it's a lot harder to make friends. That's because by then it's more difficult to show yourself as you really are; you're now more likely to feel vulnerable, and to feel that you have much more to lose, so the risk feels greater and you're tempted to continue to show mostly the good bits, the ones you hope very much will be acceptable to the other person.

Sexual attraction – what's happening?

When a man and a woman feel sexually attracted to each other, especially at the very beginning, the impact is both psychological and physical. It is as if there's electricity in the air, your whole body feels strangely awkward and very much alive at the same time. You move closer together, smiling a lot, and may even do some tentative touching. Your eyes seem to be locked and you both find it hard to look away. And, although you're talking, neither of you is taking any of it in. In addition, there are other signals, so subtle that they're only picked up subconsciously. But, subtle or obvious, you do pick them up and they tell you that this person is really interested in you. You may not understand exactly what is happening but you're very aware, both consciously and subconsciously, that something *is* happening – and so is everybody else. They know when they're not wanted!

What you've just read is a description of that 'bolt from the blue' feeling which is absolutely wonderful, but – and that's where things become more complicated and risky – when you're in the grip of this kind of feeling, you will tend to pay more attention to the things you have in common than to any differences you may have, however serious they may turn out to be. You will be eager to present yourself in the most attractive light possible, which is understandable – but please don't let it go on for too long or you will land yourself in real trouble.

There's no doubt that this a blissful and exhilarating state to be in and you're both embarking on an exciting voyage of discovery.

So I'm sexually attracted – how do I let them know?
If my workshops are anything to go by, both men and women feel a little uncertain about how to progress a relationship towards greater physical closeness. When we feel this strongly, our mind and our emotions start playing all sorts of tricks on us. Here's one example: Jo is a lovely woman, generally confident and independent, and has lots of friends in her life. She had recently met Stuart and they'd started going out together. Every time we spoke she would go on about how interesting, fun, sexy, kind, etc. etc. he was. She thought he liked her too but – and this is the interesting part – the more

aware she was of his interest, the more she began to doubt her own attractiveness. Then she started saying things such as how she was probably imagining that he was interested in her and that the whole thing was most likely wishful thinking on her part. It was as if her brain had become disconnected from her feelings. She could see he was interested, but she couldn't bring herself to really believe it. The problem was that, in order to protect herself against being rejected or hurt, she adopted a fairly distant attitude. Fortunately, Stuart wasn't easily put off and Jo got over it, but I'm mentioning it to show how vulnerable we can feel, especially at the very beginning.

Men, if a woman acts coolly towards you it may not necessarily be because she's playing hard to get. In the early days, it may be her way of trying to protect herself in case you're not really interested. There will be people out there who do play games or act in manipulative ways but I hope that you can recognise and avoid them because they could bring you all sorts of grief. Besides, you deserve better!

If you're not sure how to progress the relationship and want to test the water, there are things you can do. As a woman, you might move a shade closer, lightly touch the man's hand or arm as you talk while you look him in the eye, smiling and speaking in a soft tone of voice. Men can do this too and these things are very powerful in breaking down barriers. But, remember that they can have a devastating effect, so please use this strategy with care and only if you're really interested. *Don't do it just to tease*, that would be very unkind.

How to increase the chances of a fulfilling sex life

If the romance progresses to the point where you want to make love, you will find that the first time is likely to set the tone for the future, both in and out of bed. That's why both of you must *want* to make love rather than let yourself be pressured into it. Also, you're more likely to have a rewarding sexual relationship if the two of you are willing to talk about your feelings, your thoughts, your fears and concerns about the things that move you – both the good bits and the bad – as well as your expectations and assumptions about sex.

Over a period of time that can last hours, weeks and maybe even months, there is a sequence that gradually propels the two of you towards increasing intimacy which may end with you making love. The advantage of taking matters slowly and gradually is that either of you can stop things at any time, for example, if one of you is worried that the other is moving too fast, or if the intimacies don't feel as good as you thought they would. The reason may simply have to do with the timing – too fast, too soon – rather than with the person.

While the sequence obviously varies from couple to couple, it typically progresses from holding hands to intertwining fingers, then maybe walking closely side by side, almost touching. If you're the man, you might put your arm around the woman's waist, which tends to be regarded as a romantic bridge to more intimate and sexual touches. After that would follow taking her hand and kissing it softly, stroking her cheek, tentative and then more passionate mouth to mouth kisses while caressing face and head, fondling her breasts and other sexual touching, until you end up making love.

If you're the woman, your approach will depend on your style and what you feel comfortable doing but by the time you reach the stage where you're considering making love to this man you're likely to have already gone through some loving touches. However, if your man is a little hard of understanding and you feel fairly certain that your advances will be welcome, then locking eyes, smiling, looking at his mouth, then his eyes, then his mouth again, playing with his fingers and so on, may move things forward.

Yes, but should I?

You might be forgiven for thinking that the whole thing feels more like hard work than a romantic encounter but things are seldom straightforward and this is particularly true when it comes to dating and mating, especially with the spectre of AIDS hanging over our heads. And, on top of that, we also should be aware of the real pressures and anxieties men and women feel when they try to get together. The first thing you need to realise is that sex means different things to different people. This may sound a little strange, but people have sex for reasons that, sometimes, have little to do with love or even lust.

Marianne used to love sex and believed that, as long as she took precautions, it was OK to jump into bed on the first date. She had met Jim only recently and, as was usual with her, they very soon had sex. The problem was that lately she had begun to feel dissatisfied. 'When I first went to bed with someone,' she told me, 'I used to feel that that's what I really wanted to do, but lately I've begun to feel empty, waking up beside a virtual stranger. I haven't always gone to bed on the first date; sometimes we've gone out together for a while first, like with Jim, but we haven't really talked about anything important, and that's what is now making the sex so impersonal for me.'

But Marianne turned out to be one of the lucky ones. Jim had begun to care enough about her to realise what was going on and together they agreed to take time out to learn more about each other, what was important to them and what made them tick. When I saw Marianne next, she brought up the subject of sex again but spoke about it in a more thoughtful way. She realised, probably for the first time, the difference, as she put it, between having sex and making love.

Another example is Lorraine. Lorraine was recently divorced and her self-esteem had taken a serious battering. To her sex was proof that she was still sexually attractive.

For Philip, who had been widowed for two years, sex was a way of finding comfort and warmth in someone's arms. For him sex was a way to ease his loneliness, while Alan hasn't even thought about why he has sex. He just wants to get laid, as he puts it, as often as possible!

The point I'm trying to make here has nothing to do with what is morally right or even with safety as long as you always take precautions. In this case, the point is that you need to realise that sex means different things to different people at different times. For some, it's just a physical release, for others it might be that they really fancy this particular person, or it might be a way to show their love for them. It could be an attempt to move a relationship forwards, or a way to prove to themselves that they're still sexually attractive. Or they might have simply given in to the other person's pressure – and this is the worst possible reason to have sex.

Start by being clear about what you want, a short-term sexual relationship or something more permanent. Then discuss it openly with the other person to make sure that you're both on the same wavelength. The ideal time to talk about it is while you still have your clothes on because, once you're in the grip of passion, you certainly won't be able to think too clearly.

Your self-esteem and peace of mind depend on knowing in advance what your expectations and those of the other person are and then talking about this with them. This will increase your chances of getting what you want. If you think you would be too embarrassed to talk about it, ask yourself why you're prepared to take your clothes off and go to bed with someone you can't talk to. Besides, even if you're embarrassed, I promise you, it will be a lot less embarrassing than realising afterwards that the whole thing was just a one-night stand and a huge mistake when you thought it was the beginning of something beautiful. It's the unspoken assumption that you both want the same thing that can get you into trouble.

If you feel that matters are progressing to the point where sooner or later you will want to make love, do consider how you will bring up the subject of condoms. Don't wait until you're both so aroused that you can't think straight. You will find it helpful to work out in advance how you can word your request and this is particularly useful if you feel shy about mentioning it. Some people talk about the subject in general terms as one of many topics of conversation. All is not lost, however, even if you're caught in the heat of the moment. As a woman, you might say something along the lines of 'I really do want to make love with you, but it's very important to me that you wear a condom', and make sure that you always, but always, carry condoms with you, just in case. And, if you're a man, then all you have to do is put it on!

Do you remember that in Chapter 17, How to Recognise the Right Partner for You, I talked about observing how the other person acts? This is definitely one of the times when you need to do it. The way they respond will tell you volumes about the kind of person they generally are, how much they care about your feelings, how responsible they are, and how thoughtful. If they listen to you and take your feelings into consideration, for example, not trying to bully you into having sex without a condom or trying to make you feel inadequate if you don't want to make love just yet, then the chances are that is how they will be out of bed as well. Of course, ideally, you already know the kind of person they are before you go to bed with them.

One factor that contributes greatly to sexual happiness is that both partners are willing to ask for things or to refuse them, both in and out of bed, for example, initiating or refusing sex. On the other hand, feeling free to take the initiative is no fun if it's always one of you who is expected to do the running, because it leaves the initiator vulnerable to rejection and they may end up feeling that you don't care as much about them or that you're not as attracted to them as they are to you.

How satisfied you are sexually depends on how comfortable you both feel asking for the things you want and need, and being willing to please the other. The flip side of the coin, though, is being prepared to accept when your partner says 'no' because, after all, sex is supposed to be a source of pleasure for the two of you, as long as you don't let it become a boring routine.

In fact, asking for things or feeling able to refuse them in all areas of your relationship in a way that is clear, direct and assertive yet caring at the same time, shows not only that you respect your partner, but also that you respect yourself.

Sexual touching that works

One thing I haven't yet mentioned in this chapter is the matter of displaying affection as opposed to hinting that you want sex. The difference between the two is usually very clear to women but men often find it confusing. The main difference – and problem – between men and women is that men become physically affectionate when they want to make love while women like the affection because they like the affection, period.

In fact, both men and women want the same thing, except that they differ in the way they want it expressed. Both want to be appreciated, loved and to be made to feel lovable and special. For men, being fancied is the ultimate in romance. I recently read that men are made tender through selfless and generous sex which, by the way, does not mean lying back and thinking of England. For women, proof of love lies in cuddling, stroking, kissing and holding for its own sake. To bridge the gap, you both need to understand how the other ticks and learn to take it in turns to give each other what they need.

So, once again, let's go back to basics. You may or may not be surprised to learn that sex is actually only one part of sexual interaction. In fact, sex covers a whole range of activities from holding hands, to hugging and 'petting' and to actually making love, with or without penetration.

As with styles of loving, so it is with styles of love-making. Men and women are different in a number of ways. As a rule men can get aroused much more quickly than women. At the same time, how men and women like to be touched differs. The problem is that men tend to touch women the way they, the men, would like to be touched, and women tend to touch men the way they, the women, would like to be touched. While most men tend to like direct genital stimulation, women prefer to start love-making by being touched in non-sexual ways, everywhere *except* sex areas. This lack of understanding about how to touch the other when we make love can lead to much sexual unhappiness. To help couples improve their sexual relationship, Masters and Johnson developed a sex therapy technique that teaches couples how to touch each other's body in a way that is slow, loving, tender, gentle and playful.

When you embark on a sexual relationship you're entering unchartered waters, just as you did when you started developing your non-sexual relationship. You have to learn about each other and that involves asking your partner to tell you what feels particularly good and what isn't so hot for them. Taking it slowly, lovingly and patiently is going to be of major help towards growing a happy and fulfilling sexual relationship.

Timing

But there's more, as you knew by now there would be. Touching is only one element of a happy sexual relationship. One that is at least as important is timing. Men, this section is especially for you. You may, at times, be a little too impulsive or over-enthusiastic, making a sudden move and taking hold of your partner or patting her bottom, and expect her to be instantly turned on. A touch that feels a bit too abrupt or rough, or going straight for her genitals (even though you may have intended it to be passionate) is not as much fun for your partner as you may imagine. You may find this hard to believe because you know what's on your mind but a woman may perceive this as rather threatening. If she doesn't react as enthusiastically as you hoped, you might withdraw hurt or angry thinking she doesn't want you or your love-making. The thing is that, usually, she does but first you have to turn her on and for her this does take a little time and care. Unfortunately, because of this misunderstanding you may both end up feeling unloved.

A suggestion for you guys that will make a major difference to your love life: take your time before you get down to business. You'll love the results!

Most of these issues tend to come up once your relationship is more established, but I believe that making you aware of what might trip you up is one of the main purposes of this book. You know what they say, forewarned is forearmed!

TIPS

- Familiarise yourself with the signs that indicate interest and attraction. That way you will be able to both recognise and use them.
- Sex means different things to different people. Be clear about what you want and discuss it openly with your partner to be sure you're on the same wavelength. Your self-esteem and peace of mind depend on it.
- Women, ask your partner to wear a condom. Practise different ways of asking in the privacy of your own home so you can feel more comfortable.
- Women, pay attention to how your partner responds to your request. It will tell you everything you need to know about the kind of man he is, both in and out of bed.
- Men and women, always carry condoms with you.
- Men, always wear a condom. No exceptions!
- Learn to ask for what you want and need in a way that is not only clear, direct and assertive but also caring, both in and out of bed. This shows not only that you respect your partner but also that you respect yourself.
- Take it in turns to take the initiative. Otherwise your partner will think you don't find them as attractive as they do you.
- Both of you need to learn how to make your partner feel appreciated, loved, attractive, lovable and special. Men tend to get the message through sex and women through hugs and cuddles. Take it in turns to give each other what you need. It will do wonders for your love life.

CHAPTER 23

How to Make Love

This chapter is about the mechanics of loving but maybe not quite in the way you imagine. It's true that love is a feeling but it's also much, much more than that. Love is totally action-based and 'actions speak louder than words'. In the end it's your actions that will have consequences, more than your words and that's why they're so important. One of the consequences of expressing your love in actions is that you will not only feel more love for that person but you will also receive more love in return. I already started on this particular theme in Chapters 6 and 7, Friendship: What's it All About? and Love: An Insider's Guide when I spoke about the rules and rewards that attract and keep people in relationships. In this chapter, I'm expanding on that theme.

We all need to be told, 'I love you', 'I care about you', 'You're terrific!' 'You're important to me', 'I'm glad you're in my life!'. This is a deeply felt, fundamental need – to know that we're loved, that we're important to someone, and that they really care whether we're there or not. But such words, however important, are not enough if they're not underpinned by actions. In this chapter you will find ideas that you can use either as given, or that you can adapt; you can also add other things that suit you and the person you want to love. That person need not necessarily be your partner, it can be members of your family, friends, acquaintances and even people at work. When I talk about loving I'm actually talking about a new way of living but before you can start, you need to be aware about what you're doing already and what you're not doing so these ideas will, hopefully, also serve to 'wake you up'.

First of all, the most important person to start showing your affection to is *yourself*. Are you surprised? You shouldn't be. The cost of not caring about yourself is heavy. If you don't care about yourself you will do two things that are guaranteed to ruin your relationship:

1. You will find it hard to accept love because you will feel undeserving, and this will make you unconsciously sabotage your relationships in subtle but lethal ways.
2. You will tend to believe that there's a limited amount of love to go around and you're likely to stick to the rule that you both have to give 50-50. If you give 'X' amount of love, then you must get 'Y' amount of love back, and you will stop giving it until you think that the balance between your give and take has been restored. And you will usually wait for the other person to start.

The truth is that it is not just hard to love other people if you don't think much of yourself, in fact, it's impossible. That's why I've devoted a whole chapter to helping you learn how to be your own best friend (Chapter 24, How to Care for Yourself: The Magic of Self-Esteem).

This chapter, however, is devoted to showing you how you can express your affection for others, first in fairly general terms, and then with more specific ideas.

1. Nothing, but nothing, makes a person feel more loved than being truly listened to, the kind of listening that helps you understand this person deeply, where they're coming from, their deepest anxieties and vulnerabilities, and still accept them as they are. That's what makes the other person feel understood, affirmed, valued, validated and appreciated – all at once. If you look inside your heart and listen to your own feelings and past hurts, you will know that the scars

you carry around with you have to do with not having been heard, maybe even since your childhood. That's a heavy burden. When you don't feel heard, then it 'follows' that you're not worth hearing, you're not a worthwhile person, not good enough. When you recognise how painful it is not to be heard, then you will know what an amazingly powerful gift you have in you to give by listening. When you listen to someone, you heal them, you make them whole again. Re-read Chapter 19, Listening – The Ultimate Aphrodisiac.

2. Keep on tuning into the things you value, respect and admire about another person. Keep listening to the music!

3. Express these things in specific terms as soon as you notice whatever it is that they've said or done, or anything you notice that fills your heart with pride and affection. Don't let that moment pass. It will never return! Life can be full of missed opportunities – if you let it. Don't let it!

4. By the same token, stop nagging and criticising. It will only damage your relationship. Re-read Chapter 20, In Praise of Praise. It covers both this and the previous point.

5. Express your affection non-verbally by looking at them, smiling at them with warmth in your eyes, or with a touch. Re-read Chapter 21, The Power of Touch.

6. Do those little thoughtful things that keep you in touch with your partner's feelings. One way that will help you think of ideas is to put yourself in their shoes. How would you feel if you were in their position? Here's just one example: If you're going to be late, phone to let them know. Don't assume that they will guess what's happened. Look at it from their point of view. What would go through your head if your partner didn't call to let you know that they're going to be late? Would you worry in case they were involved in an accident? Do you wish you knew how long you have to wait so you can decide whether to have your dinner now or wait until their

return? Or would you think, 'I really should know why they're late and not worry. It's really stupid of me. I won't think about the clock ticking away or the fact that they're two hours late.'

Often, because things are clear to us, we imagine that they're clear to everybody else. This crystal ball approach to relationships is deadly. There are better ways.

7. Do *not* try to change your partner. There are lots of reasons for this. For one, it doesn't work and only brings out that rebellious streak in them ('I'll do it just to annoy them!'). But, worse, it makes them feel angry, resentful, worthless, not good enough for you. And it is extraordinarily damaging – not only to themselves but also to you and your relationship.

8. Ask them for help. An important way of showing how much you value the other person is to turn to them in time of need and to trust them to be there for you.

9. Offer your support without necessarily waiting to be asked. Sometimes they will accept it, sometimes they won't but they will know that you're there for them, should they need you. It's extraordinarily important to know that we're not alone and, when you offer them your support, either your shoulder or practical help, they will know it and that's enormously comforting.

That help can even be the seemingly mundane, such as doing the washing up (not just offering to help but doing it without asking or waiting to be asked), or something like supporting them both emotionally and practically when they want to do an Open University course. One is not bigger than the other. Both are important ways of showing your love.

10. Don't show disapproval if your partner disagrees with you. You're not clones of each other. Accept gracefully that, since you've both been exposed to different experiences, it's OK to be different in the ways you both think and feel.

11. Don't judge them. That's a dangerous and damaging thing to do.
12. Be straight yet caring with them. It's not honest to tell them a few home truths – it's vengeance. Being straight is to tell them the truth, and not just what they want to hear. We're all masters at self-deception and self-sabotage. Let me give you an example. Say you have a friend who's trying to lose weight and who keeps moaning, 'I hardly have anything to eat! I don't know why I'm stuck!' You bump into them on a hot day having an ice cream, and they say, 'I felt I really deserved this! Besides, I've lost a pound! And anyway, it's so hot!' How do you react? Do you say, 'Good for you for having lost that pound! Of course you deserve this ice cream! It's such a lovely sunny day!'? Or do you say, 'Good for you for losing that pound! But this ice cream is sabotaging your efforts. Don't do that. If you need support to resist temptation, I'm here but don't try to fool yourself. I won't let you!' Yes, they may get upset that you saw through them and that they didn't get away with it, and they may even take it out on you. But friends, including partners and lovers, don't take the easy way out.
13. Buy a bottle of wine . . . just because.
14. Buy them a little gift, for no reason at all.
15. Do more than your fair share. One of the things that causes strain in relationships is a perceived unequal share of responsibilities. In successful relationships there's not – as most people believe – a 50-50 per cent split in responsibilities. In successful relationships *both partners give 100 per cent*.
16. Have an affectionate pet name for them.
17. Call them when you're away.
18. Send them a little love note.
19. Cook them a special meal. That's usually more valued if it's done by the person who doesn't normally cook.

20. Make time to do enjoyable things together. Give your partner all of yourself, and by that I mean give them your time and your whole attention at frequent intervals rather than expecting them to accept that you work seventy hours a week for them. The key here is balance, not one extreme or the other. If you remember Chapter 11, Men and Women: What Do We Want from each Other?, number one on the women's list was 'generous with his time . . .' When you do fun things together you will avoid one of the main traps that destroys relationships: boredom. Here are some ideas:

a) Go to see a film that you both enjoy.
b) Go out for a meal. Play footsie.
c) Have a picnic somewhere – the more secluded the spot, the better. Feed each other.
d) Get a video and a take-away. There's no law that says you can't cuddle at the same time.
e) Go for a walk hand-in-hand.
f) Sit together in the park.
g) Ask them what would make them happy, and then do it (read Chapter 26, Laughter: The Missing Link).

Use your creativity to come up with other ideas. Invest in your relationships and you will be rewarded a thousand-fold.

TIPS
- Hearing love *words* is very important but they need to be backed by love *acts*. This will enable you to feel more for that person, and to receive love back.
- The most important person you need to show affection to is yourself.
- Take action. Do things that will let the other person know that you love and care about them.

CHAPTER 24

How to Care for Yourself:
The Magic of Self-Esteem

One important element that can make or break our relationship is whether or not we have a good level of self-esteem. There are a number of reasons for this. If we feel lovable and deserving of happiness, then we're more likely to choose a partner that will reflect and support our own view of ourselves. If, on the other hand, we feel inadequate, unlovable and undeserving of happiness, then we're more likely to become involved with someone who will confirm this negative belief about ourselves. Of course, I know that no one would deliberately go out and choose someone who will treat them badly. It happens because these beliefs are so deeply buried inside us that we're often not even aware that we hold them. Furthermore, if we think well of ourselves, then we're more likely to treat our partner well and to expect them to treat us well in return. Either way, it's a self-fulfilling prophecy.

There's another reason why self-esteem has such a deep impact on our relationships. If we feel that we're basically OK, then we won't be afraid to show ourselves as we really are which means that we're able to create intimate relationships. If we have poor self-esteem then we just couldn't do that. We'd be too afraid that, if we showed ourselves as we really are, we would be seen as unacceptable and be rejected. It's a vicious circle. With love, however, we cannot play it safe, we have to take the risk of making ourselves open and vulnerable, which is why we need to know that we're lovable and worthwhile.

237

Self-esteem is also one of the qualities of happy people. It's the quality that enables us to say a wholehearted YES to life and all it has to offer, it helps us take control and make things happen, approach people and make friends with them, and finally, it enables us to deal with rejection as well as with the fear of it.

Of course, even people with high self-esteem will occasionally suffer self-doubts but, on balance, what makes it easier for them to meet lots of people and make lots of friends is the fact that they're more relaxed, more casual about meeting people, less self-conscious, more open, more friendly and more approachable. They genuinely enjoy meeting people and they don't take it so seriously when someone doesn't respond to them. They know that, sooner or later, someone else will!

I bet you're thinking, 'If I were more relaxed and less self-conscious, I wouldn't be sitting here reading this book.' I can understand that. Being out there, meeting new people and making new friends means that we're putting ourselves on the line and it's inevitable that, sooner or later, we will get rejected. I have covered the topic of rejection at length in Chapters 2 and 3, so I won't go into it again except to say that, with rejection, there are two issues:

1. the fear of rejection
2. the actual rejection.

It's the fear of rejection that paralyses us and stops us from going up to people, while the actual rejection can fuel future fear of rejection which then stops us from approaching people, in a never-ending vicious circle.

Earlier on I said that inside our confident exterior is a scared individual wondering if we're good enough, likeable enough, lovable enough. Unless we believe we are, it will be difficult to persuade anybody else.

Unfortunately, people with low self-esteem tend to try very

hard to be liked by everyone, wanting to be all things to all people, afraid that, if they express an opinion that's different, people will take offence. In fact, nothing could be further from the truth. 'Yes-people' are seen as boring and people feel uncomfortable with them. For more on this, see Chapter 16, How to Avoid Being a Bore.

A few years ago, after Hazel had been made redundant, she was at a crossroads trying to decide between looking for another job and becoming self-employed. 'Just as I'd almost made up my mind to become self-employed,' she told me, 'I was invited to attend a job interview so I decided to leave my future up to fate. I thought the interview had gone really well,' she went on, 'so I was really peeved when I wasn't even invited for a second interview. I rang up the interviewer and asked him if he could tell me why I hadn't been shortlisted. To his credit, this man was honest with me.' Hazel paused and then went on, 'He told me that I had come across as a very strong and confident woman and that the partners in that firm would have been too intimidated by me! I thanked him and said that next time I would tone it down. Then he said something I've never forgotten. He said: "Don't do that! If you get a job by pretending to be someone different from who you really are, you will end up being unhappy and in the wrong job." ' To her credit, Hazel took the advice and applied it not only to her career (she now runs her own business), but to her private life as well.

Self-esteem and a sense of one's own worth are things that people put very high on their list of priorities. In fact, the need is so great that it has become a major industry! Individual counselling, courses, and lots and lots of books can all be very valuable in giving us that necessary kick-start, but no course or book or anybody else can give us our sense of self-esteem. Only we can do that – which is what this chapter is about.

There are people who say that it's not what you do that makes you worthwhile but who you are, that you are worthwhile because you're a human being. Though it sounds appealing it is only part of the story. The whole story is that it's not only *what* we do but *how* we do what we do and how we live our life that will help us grow our own sense of self worth. The ingredients I would include are kindness, a sense of honour and integrity, courage to take risks and to stand up for what we believe in, persistence and not taking the easy way out – our underlying philosophy of how we face life and how we treat ourselves and other people. It is not easy, but that just makes it more valuable.

More often than not we go through life without ever discovering what we're really made of; we think of ourselves as victims of fate, we whinge, we complain, we kick others or we kick the cat whenever things don't go our way, we blame our parents and other people for holding us back, and spend much time and energy coming up with very creative reasons why we're stuck in a rut. This is a victim mentality and it takes as much effort to talk ourselves into that frame of mind as it does to talk ourselves out of it.

You need to find out who you really are, and to do that you need to test and stretch yourself. Putting yourself in new situations, learning and trying out new things can be an extremely exhilarating though sometimes scary way of doing that. But choose areas that truly interest you. If you don't know whether or not you're going to like something, then give it a go and see how you feel about it. If you like it, great. Even if you don't, don't give up straight away. Hang in there for a while longer and give it a fair try. You might discover a lot of things, not least about yourself, such as the fact that you don't run away at the smallest difficulty, or that you're persistent.

Nothing that comes too easily will give you such a powerful sense of accomplishment as something that you find difficult but persevere at. Let me give you two examples:·

EXAMPLE 1
Today I'm a Fellow of the Institute of Personnel and Development. Although of course I'm very pleased with it, it was in fact

achieving my first rung on the ladder of professional qualifications that gave me the most amazing sense of accomplishment.

I'd left school at the age of fourteen and spent more than fifteen years working as a secretary. In 1976 I felt I'd reached a crossroads and decided that the time was right for me to change careers. After looking into various options I decided that I wanted to get into personnel management. However, I had a lot of catching up to do first, so I went back to school with sixteen- and seventeen-year-olds to do 'O' and 'A' levels and then a postgraduate diploma in Personnel Administration.

I discovered – afterwards – that it didn't give me the coveted letters after my name which would have equipped me with the necessary credibility when applying for jobs. With the combination of no experience in the profession and no letters after my name, the odds against my entering the personnel management field were high.

Having decided three years previously that the time was right to move out of secretarial work and to change career direction, I now found myself having to return to it in order to survive. Let me tell you, I was bitterly disappointed! I also was 'clever' enough to 'choose' a boss who didn't like secretaries who didn't want to be secretaries. That meant that I had to do my studying in secret, getting up at four in the morning to study, then go to work and continue studying afterwards. Obviously, there's no way I could have done it without my family's support, but it still wasn't exactly a piece of cake.

That's why sitting that particular set of examinations and getting to that first rung feels to me like such a stunning achievement. And it was because of – not despite – the fact that it was so hard for me that I treasure it so much.

EXAMPLE 2
This second example has to do with the fact that today I'm earning my living doing the one thing I used to be most afraid

of: standing up in front of a group of people, giving talks and seminars and running workshops. And what I discovered was not only that I'm good at it but also that it gives me the greatest thrill.

Do you think I would ever have found that out if I'd given up just because my tummy seized up in terror whenever I had to stand up and give an assignment? Honestly, it wasn't that I have a masochistic streak in me, but that I knew that it was something I had to learn to deal with if I wanted to move forward and grow.

People who cop out – because that's what it is – when things get tough are generally the kind of people who, for example, may end up having, instead of ten years' experience, only one year's experience ten times. You need to continue to learn and change and grow. If you don't, you will be left behind. Nowhere is this more clearly visible than in the world of work where people are being made redundant but are unable to meet the market's demands because their skills are out of date. So let your willingness to learn and grow become second nature to you. Besides, our accomplishments pave the way for other successes and they, in turn, feed our confidence and self-esteem.

Things get even better. These actions, be they learning new skills as a hobby or to increase our marketability, or going out and approaching new people tend to generate positive reactions in others which, in turn, affects the way we feel about ourselves and about our own limitations (which are now fewer than we used to think). This then encourages us to continue taking up other interests, and getting involved with other things – all in an upward spiral.

I have more ideas for you to consider and try out. They are extremely powerful and they work provided, of course, that you put them into practice and keep at it. Make them into a programme. More than that, make a habit of them, make them a part of you and your life.

Give your life a kick-start!

Feeling good about ourselves starts with good health, eating well, sleeping enough, drinking and smoking only in moderation, if at all. This may sound boring but the reason I mention it is because health and vitality act like a magnet. So, have a look at what you eat, how many hours sleep you need, make some exercise part of your normal day and learn to manage your stress levels. There's more on how to do this in Chapter 25, The Art of Being Happy.

Is this the best you can look?

Knowing we look our best will also increase our self-confidence. Thinking about how we would like people to see us (which will obviously vary depending on the situation), and then asking ourselves if the way we dress conveys that image is a good way to start. You may find it worth re-reading Chapter 10, What Attracts People to One Another? Ask yourself: 'Do people see me as somebody who just throws on whatever is nearest or am I happy that they see what I want them to see?' If you're not sure, ask someone you really trust or, even better, invest in personal advice from an image consultant on how to look the best 'you' you possibly can. Look for advertisements in women's magazines.

This doesn't mean that you have to look as if you're about to step on to a catwalk. The reason I've included this point is because many of us – men and women – often act on automatic, seldom giving this area any thought at all. I'm here to ask you the questions and to awaken your self-awareness. You can then decide what to do about it.

Take up new activities

All too often we do the same things, in the same way, with the same people, day in and day out, year in and year out. In short, we get into a rut. That's why we need to make a conscious effort to get out of it. Doing this will have a number of results:

we will begin to see ourselves in a different and more positive light, we will have new experiences and we will meet new people.

Here are some ideas that might work for you and help you make a start. They may seem very small but they are designed to make you see yourself and your world with fresh eyes. Any change will do! For example:

- If you always go for lunch with someone from your department ask a colleague from another.
- If you can, change your lunch hour and/or the place where you have your lunch. That way you will see new faces.
- If you always buy the same perfume or after-shave lotion, try a new one.
- If you always stick to the same clothes style or colours, try out something new. Get rid of your blinkers! Don't decide in advance what will or will not suit you. Experiment a little by trying on new things. You don't have to buy them. Perhaps you would feel more comfortable trying out different colour scarves and putting them on in new ways. The shop assistant will usually be glad to help. Or try on skirts that are longer or shorter than the ones you normally wear; or perhaps try a different neckline. Take it slowly but keep an open mind. The idea is to become the best 'you' you possibly can.
- Try out new make-up offered free by cosmetic counters in big department stores and ask the assistant to show you how to do it.
- If you wear spectacles, then frames can be a wonderful fashion accessory. I wear them and I love what they do for me.
- Do something – anything! – just for yourself on a regular basis. For example, have a leisurely bubble bath; have an aromatherapy massage; go for a walk in the countryside; pretend you're a tourist even if you're been living in the area for the last twenty years so you can see it all with fresh eyes;

go to the cinema or theatre either on your own or with a friend. The point here is not necessarily to meet someone but to do something that makes you feel good – and the more 'decadent' the better. (By the way, by decadent I mean anything pampering and indulgent, and that makes you feel great.) You deserve it!

- Take up a new hobby or interest.
- Enrol in some evening classes to develop a new skill, re-train for a new type of job or career or simply learn something new and enjoyable like photography, painting, tennis, flower arranging, flying, parachuting, clowning skills for charity, or whatever appeals to you. Watch out for ads in the various magazines.
- Join amateur dramatics or your local gym.
- Join Friends of the Earth.
- Go on an activity weekend. There are some really original ones around, like 'Murder Weekends' where you can play detective, or 'Period Weekends' where you can dress up in the appropriate style.

Even if you're one of those people who don't like doing things on their own try anyway. Don't wait for that wonderful person to come along so you can start sharing experiences and doing things together. Start doing your own thing – you won't believe the difference it will make to you and your life when you become involved in something – anything – that engages your mind and your heart! If you're not sure what you'd like to do, start by trying things out, experiment a little. How do you know you won't like it until you've tried it?

Begin gradually to build an interesting life for yourself which includes doing things for and by yourself as well as with other people and you will discover not only that you can have fun even if you're on your own but you will also become the kind of person that attracts other people.

Make your life more balanced

If you're one of those people who have, for example, become single-minded about one aspect of their life, restore the balance. Yes, there *is* life after work!

If you're not sure if your life is out of balance then try this exercise which comes in two stages.

STAGE 1

Take a blank sheet of paper and head it with the number 168 which represents one whole week (24 hours times 7 days). Now take away the number of hours you spend sleeping, e.g. 49 (7 hours times 7 days) – which leaves you with 119 hours, then take away the number of hours you spend working during the week, including the time it takes to travel to and from work, and take that away from 119. Now continue to take away your other time commitments such as home managing duties, and so on, noting each activity separately with the number of hours you spend on that activity and deduct it from the previously remaining number of hours.

STAGE 2

Look over your list very carefully and ask yourself three questions:

1. Which activities are absolutely essential and which are not?
2. Of the ones that are not critical, which do I really enjoy and which are just a burden?
3. Of the ones that are not critical and which are just a burden, are there any I can drop?

We often do things just because we've always done them, even though the need for them no longer exists. That means that it's worth investing a little time to make sure that we make the best possible use of all our available time. What I mean by best possible use is having as balanced a life as we possibly can. So, even in the unlikely event that you decide that there are no activities that you can drop, you can still ask yourself these further three questions:

1. Do I devote too much time to this activity?
2. Could someone else occasionally share the burden?
3. Could I do it differently and more quickly?

To inject balance into your life you need to have a mix of activities, for example, time spent with friends and family; going out and socialising; being engaged in some hobby or other interests; learning new things; time for solitude and reflection, which can be enormously energising; and so on. Whatever you're engaged in, give it all you've got. Don't do anything in a half-hearted way, with your mind elsewhere. That would be a terrible waste. It's the difference between just existing and really living!

Surround yourself with positive and supportive people

Surround yourself with people who encourage and believe in you. There are too many people out there whingeing, complaining, criticising, putting people down and inviting you to join them in their misery. Such people have no place in your life! I have suggested elsewhere how you can create a positive, accepting environment so people will want to be with you, and the same applies the other way round. Avoid people who try to drag you down with them and don't ever let anyone put you down. As you learn to really like and accept yourself as you are, you will notice that others will begin to take you at your own valuation; when people take the liberty of putting you down, they're also taking you at your own valuation. If you're just beginning your 'journey' and have difficulty handling put-downs and asking for what you want, then enrol in one of those assertiveness skills courses. They're very helpful in developing not just the skills but also the confidence to put them into practice.

It isn't always easy to get your existing friends to change the way they treat you, and I don't recommend that you give them an ultimatum. What I suggest you do is sit down with them and explain what kind of life you want to lead, namely one that is optimistic, hopeful, warm and loving, where put-downs and sniping, criticism and sarcasm have no place. Ask them to support you in this and to help you to get rid of old negative habits. Tell them you need all the help and support you can get and that you would like to have theirs. Ask for help and you're very likely to get it.

However, if they can't or won't support you, use your assertiveness skills to make it clear to them what you will and will not tolerate. If all else fails you may need to review your friendship with this person. In some cases all you will have to do is just let it fizzle out. In others you may have to confront them with their persistent negative habits after you've tried your best, and explain that you can't afford to continue the friendship because the 'costs' are too high.

Homework

For one whole week try the following:

- Do not complain about a single thing! Instead, use 'winner's talk', that is talking about things, your life, your job, your family and your friends in positive terms.
- Keep a record of every wonderful little thing that happens to you every day, from finding a parking place without any hassle to someone saying something nice to you; from how pleasant the sun feels on your face to how good your sandwich tastes; or even the pleasant chat you had with the milkman.

It doesn't really matter how trivial it seems. The chances of a major earth-shaking event happening such as winning the pools are not too high so you had better learn to enjoy the small things in life. If you do this, you're much more likely to become a great deal happier. (See Chapter 25, The Art of Being Happy.) Record every single incident. The idea is to make you aware of how many pleasant things actually happen which we tend to take for granted, and the reason I'm asking you to write them down is three-fold.

1. It helps you get into a regular practice so it becomes easier to develop the habit of noticing the many little beautiful things all around you.
2. It reinforces the experience.
3. It makes it last longer because you can go back, re-read the previous day's or week's entries and re-experience the good feelings.

- Following on from the previous exercise, choose one day of your life to make a written record of every humorous and joyful event, witticism, joke you hear, any unexpected 'funnies' you come across or anything at all that makes you chuckle. Do this once, twice, three times and you will find that if you look for humour, humour will find you. Laughing at yourself and laughing at life is a really attractive quality that people appreciate.
- Spoil yourself! Prescribe yourself a treat, a reward, a gift, a little luxury. Look around you with fresh eyes. Pretend you're a visitor from Mars or, better yet, a child. Admire a blossom, smell a rose, acknowledge the wisdom of a child, a friend, or your own thoughts, buy a favourite magazine, enjoy a walk in the park, watch the sun set or rise – alone or with somebody else, admire the stars or the full moon.

What happens when you begin to do these things is that you gradually become someone who's even more interesting and more fun to be with, and that's when you don't just start to attract people but you start to attract the right kind of people, people who are fun, friendly, kind, interesting and supportive. We are all put off by people who're needy or bored, the kind that looks to others to make them happy, but we're all attracted to people who enjoy life because they are a joy to be with.

TIPS

- Put yourself in new situations, learn and try out new things – but choose areas that you think will interest you. Experiment! Some things you will enjoy and some you won't but you won't know which is which until you try.
- If you find something that you think is too hard, do not give up straight away. Give it a fair try.
- Look after your health. Make sure you eat well, sleep enough, do some exercise, and drink and smoke only in moderation.
- Ask yourself: 'Is this the best I can look?' 'Is this how I want people to see me?' and if the answer to either question is 'no', do something about it.
- Create balance in your life. Let it include not only work but also your personal time, hobbies, family and friends. Give each of these areas all you've got!
- Surround yourself with positive and supportive people.
- Do your homework.

CHAPTER 25

The Art of Being Happy

I bet you didn't know that you can actually learn to be happy. I bet you thought that happiness was something that happens to you if you're lucky, and that generally you only realise you were happy after it is all over and you're not happy any more. Well, I have news for you. Not only can you learn to be happy, I'm going to show you how.

First of all, let's start with what happiness is not. Happiness is not when you don't have any problems. If you ever thought you will be happy when something happens or stops happening, then forget it. The time to be happy is now!

Yes, I know you're thinking, 'Of course I want to be happy! Doesn't everybody? But how? What do I have to do?' The answer is that happiness starts with a decision. The first thing you have to do is *decide to be happy*. No, I'm not having you on. Really!

Happiness is a subjective feeling, a very personal thing. You might be happy in circumstances in which other people might be unhappy. You're happy when you feel that your life as a whole is fulfilling, meaningful and pleasant. Happiness is a deep and on-going sense that all will be well, in spite of that day's disappointments and frustrations.

Let me give you the results of recent research into happiness. You will find them fascinating.

Factors that do not make any difference to how happy we are

Let's start by looking at the things that make no difference either way, that is, if you have this or suffer that, it makes no difference whatsoever as to how happy or miserable you are. For example:

- Having money does not make us either happy or unhappy. Happiness is unrelated to how much money we have.
- Strokes of good luck make no difference to how happy we are. It's true that getting a pay rise, a promotion, winning a game, or winning the pools makes us feel terrific – but only for a while.
- Day-to-day frustrations make no difference to how miserable we are either. Of course, having an argument, being rejected, having a headache, or being turned down for promotion make us feel despondent, but that's also temporary.

  In both the last two cases we will soon be back to normal, whether it's back to our usual gloomy or our usual happy self.
- Our level of happiness is not affected by whether we are a man or a woman, black or white, young or old. It's our *attitude* to these factors that makes the difference.
- Being disabled doesn't mean that we also have to be unhappy or unfulfilled; even being in a horrific accident doesn't mean that we will never be happy again.

What does make a difference is how we compare ourselves to other people and our expectations. For example, if we constantly compare ourselves with the Joneses then we're bound to be discontented, dissatisfied and unhappy. People who have unrealistic expectations are guaranteed to be disappointed most of the time.

What kinds of people are happy?

Before trying to answer the question 'How can I be happy?',

let's look at what kinds of people are happy. People who are happy have four inner qualities:

1. They have a healthy sense of self-esteem
2. They're basically optimistic
3. They're outgoing
4. They have a sense of being in control of their lives.

Let's take a brief look at each of these qualities.

1. *Happy people like themselves* They know they're basically likeable and lovable. They also know that, occasionally, they will mess up and, although they may find it frustrating, they know that it doesn't take away from their intrinsic worth.
2. *Happy people are optimistic and hopeful* Basically that means that, if you think in negative terms, you're more likely to get negative results. If you think in positive terms, you're more likely to get positive results. Two thousand years ago Virgil wrote the same law in the *Aeneid*: 'They can because they think they can.' Happy people are those that approach life with an attitude that says YES! to possibilities and opportunities.

   However, the research in this area adds a word of caution: healthy optimists take sensible precautions and plan steps in case things don't work out as they hoped. They have a fall-back position or, in business terms, they do 'contingency planning'. The idea is to do what we can to reduce the risk and mitigate any losses we may experience.
3. *Happy people are outgoing* Extroverts are cheerful people. Cheerful people are more likely to like themselves, and are confident that other people will like them too. Such convictions tend to be self-fulfilling (as are negative convictions) and that's why happy people seem to experience more pleasant events. As a rule outgoing people tend to have close friends, good jobs and be married.

The reason is clear: if you're outgoing, then you're more likely to go out and meet people, so people like to have you around. The bottom line is that outgoing people have a stronger support system which is one of the fundamental elements to our sense of well-being.

Please don't let all this make you feel discouraged. These are all qualities you can develop. You may not have been born with an outgoing personality but, by following the practical suggestions later on in this chapter, you can learn new things that will enable you to become more outgoing than you are today. But you do have to give them a proper go!

4. *Happy people choose their own destinies* That means that they know where they're going. It means that they have goals and objectives, and that they're taking steps that will get them there. But that's not all. Being in control also means being able to make decisions that affect them. That's why in a work situation, for example, operating machines can be such an alienating experience. Or some old people's homes, where they have no say in what happens to them. Basically, happy people can decide how to use their time. Drifting leads to depression, a sense of powerlessness and lack of meaning.

Happy people are more attractive because they're more fun to be with than grumpy or depressed people. Happy people are more trusting, more compassionate and more focused on other people. They are the kind of people who are more able to form happy and lasting relationships – from friendship to love.

'That's all very well', I hear you say, 'but how can I get a bit of that?'

How can we become more optimistic, more in control, more outgoing and like ourselves better?

It's true that we already come into the world with many of these characteristics, but it's equally true that we can change our own destiny – if we choose to do so. In fact, *what we do today affects what tomorrow looks like for us*. This is a critically important message yet few people realise the full implications.

Most people believe that our attitudes influence our behaviour. Although that's true to some extent, it's less true than we have tended to believe. Here, then, is the magic formula:

WE CAN ACT OURSELVES INTO A NEW WAY OF THINKING.

The truth is that it's mostly our behaviour that influences our attitudes. But this is a gradual process. Actions and attitudes feed on and affect each other in an ever-increasing spiral. It is true for changing people into evil creatures such as happened in Nazi Germany, and it's equally true for changing ourselves into happier and more confident individuals. This is how we can do it:

• *Act as if* If, for example, you want to become a kinder, more confident, and more outgoing person, then what you do is you *act as if*. This means that you have to pretend to be the kind of person you want to become by *acting as if* you already were that kind of person. I often describe the process as 'You don't have to *be* Hamlet to *play* Hamlet', except that actors usually take on the personality and qualities of the character they're playing, at least for the duration of the play.

  If all this sounds frivolous, don't be fooled. Social psychologists have discovered that moods – either a good mood or a bad mood – are enhanced by acting and talking in that mode so, for example, complaining actually makes you feel even more discontented, while talking in positive terms makes you feel good. On the basis of these results, they have developed two related techniques: 'Acting As If' which I've just described, and 'Saying-Becomes-Believing' which encourages people to talk about themselves, their job, their friends and their life, in generally positive terms. Both these techniques, acting and talking, are widely used in various types of therapies.

Yes, I know you're thinking, 'The whole thing sounds phoney to me.' I can understand that. But, believe me, the phoniness is only temporary. Whenever we move into a new role, for example when we become a new Mum or a new Dad, get our first job after having been a student, are promoted into a new position, or become a mature student, we feel uncomfortable and unsure about how we should act. But gradually, as we become more familiar with new ways of behaving, we begin to feel more comfortable in our new role and the new attitudes that go with that role. To use an analogy, it's like wearing in a pair of new shoes until they feel really comfortable.

But, as with the shoes, these changes don't happen overnight. What does *acting as if* look like in practice? Here are some examples.

1. If you want to become more confident, look the other person in the eye, use a firm tone of voice, have a friendly expression on your face, hold your body straight, and finish your sentences instead of letting them trail off.

2. If you want to become more cheerful, put on a happy face, as the song says, Phoney? Corny? Maybe. But it works. Not only does it make you feel happier, it makes the people around you feel better too.

3. If you want to feel more hopeful and optimistic, start by walking at a purposeful pace, in long strides, taking deep breaths, swinging your arms, having a friendly expression on your face, and looking ahead, as if you had an important place to get to. If you think this is too simple, then try walking with short shuffling steps, taking shallow breaths, with a gloomy expression on your face and

with your eyes downcast. Can you feel the difference in your mood?

4. If you want to become more outgoing, go over to that person and say 'Hello, I'm Madeline Bates. What's your name?' and take it from there. Re-read Chapter 18, What Do You say After You Say 'Hello'?

5. If you want to become kinder, *act as if* you knew that people yearn for friendliness and affection, then *do* acts of kindness, large or small, it doesn't matter.

6. If you want to feel happier, start *acting as if* you were happy. How do happy people act? They smile more, they talk more about happy or positive topics, they move in a more determined way, they do more things they enjoy.

- *Set targets*   This is a powerful way of turning boredom into enjoyment. Set yourself challenges. If you're a middling darts player, decide to become really good at the game, and set yourself a realistic deadline. Then monitor your progress. Make a decision to improve at least one of your skills. When you've accomplished that move on to something else. It will keep you focused, learning and achieving new things, which in turn will keep you young and enthusiastic.

- *Pursue a dream*   A goal is a dream with a deadline. To start you dreaming, ask yourself: if you were to die tomorrow, what would you regret most not having done? What did you dream of becoming when you grew up? It's not as absurd as you might think. As I'm writing this paragraph, I remember that when I was little I wanted to become a filmstar so I could get to kiss Cary Grant. Although today I'm not a filmstar, I do have a stage of my own: my workshops. Maybe your dream can be adapted to suit who you are today? What do you love doing in your spare time? Are you a secret painter? Do you love taking photographs? What! You're not good enough to have an exhibition? Why not work towards it? After all, you don't have to be in the Tate

Gallery – or maybe you do? Invest time and think about it!

- *Take more risks!* Try out new things, let yourself make more mistakes! Remember, the person who never makes a mistake never makes anything.

- *Enjoy the present moment* Become aware of your surroundings. We're living at a pace that is much too hurried. Life is passing us by and we hardly know it. We have stopped noticing the stars, the sunset, the blossoms and the trees, the smell of freshly mown grass, and the fact that the sun is shining. When you go shopping, do you notice the smell of freshly baked bread? Some bakeries bake bread on the premises, even supermarkets,· and they have this delicious smell. And have you noticed the smell of spices when you enter a health food store? Or acknowledged lovers kissing, or a mother or father playing with their baby? Or watched a spider spinning its web? That's really something to behold!

- *Stop acting on 'automatic'* Wake up! Be 'there' one hundred per cent, irrespective of what you're doing.

- *Look at how you use your free time* Use it purposefully. Don't waste it by flopping in front of the telly. If your excuse is that you're tired then I have news for you. Sitting in front of the telly, like a couch potato, is going to make you even more tired and your batteries will become completely flat.

    Remember how bored and listless I felt when my Dad asked me to help Mum with the dishes and how quickly I perked up when he added that afterwards we'd go to the cinema? This works on the same principle. Do something that totally absorbs you and you won't believe how energetic you will feel.

- *Learn to reduce your stress levels* Here's how to do it:

1. Take relaxing walks in the park or countryside, or taking the side streets to avoid the busy main roads
2. Smile at people

3. Talk with friends
4. See the funny side of life
5. Only worry about things you can do something about. Why waste your energies anticipating the terrible things that might never happen?
6. Develop your spirituality or religious faith, whatever it may be.

There's plenty of advice available in books on exercise, nutrition, sleep and various kinds of relaxation techniques, all of which will add to your sense of well-being.

- *Be kind to others*   You'll be surprised at how powerful this is. Being kind to other people comes back to you a hundred-fold.
- *Have more fun!*   Treat yourself on ice cream or other child-like pleasures more often.
- *Let yourself be silly from time to time!*   This is not the same as being irresponsible. It's not taking yourself too seriously. People who live sensibly, seriously and sanely all the time grow old quicker.

I'm sure you can come up with lots of ideas of your own. Make a list of as many things as possible that will make today better than you thought it was going to be, things that make your heart sing. The last time I made a list I came up with:

- sharing a bottle of Mateus Rosé wine with strawberries with thick Greek yogurt with someone special
- sharing a funny experience with somebody
- listening to my favourite music (the type of music depends on my mood at the time)
- watching a funny film or hiring a funny video
- reading something I find engrossing
- preparing my Mum's chocolate cake for a special friend

- going strawberry-picking with friends
- walking in the countryside
- phoning a friend
- hugging a friend or being hugged (I can never decide which I like better)
- having a massage.

I bet next time I make another list it will contain different things. Get started, draw up your own list, and then put the ideas into practice.

Furthermore, two other things – a network of supportive, affectionate friends and a fulfilling love life – will ensure that:

1. You suffer fewer illnesses
2. You recover more quickly when you do fall sick
3. You're better able to manage the ups and downs of life
4. You have more confidence and higher self-esteem.

That's what this book is all about. And it's also about *you* taking control, taking the initiative and making things happen. Remember that being in control is one of the elements that promotes happiness.

TIPS
- Use both techniques, 'Act As If' and 'Saying-Becomes-Believing', to put yourself into a positive frame of mind
- Set targets
- Pursue a dream
- Take more risks!
- Enjoy the present moment
- Stop acting on 'automatic'
- Look at how you use your free time
- Learn to reduce your stress levels
- Be kind to others

- Have more fun!
- Let yourself be silly from time to time!
- List as many ideas as possible of the many different ways you can make today much better than you thought it would be. Head your list 'To Make Today Truly Terrific I will . . .'

CHAPTER 26

Laughter: The Missing Link

Not all that long ago you might have had a doctor dismissing your physical symptoms as just being 'all in the mind'. Over the past fifty years, however, there has been an enormous amount of research into how negative emotions such as anger, anxiety, depression and fear damage health and delay recovery. In response to all that evidence, a number of scientists began to ask themselves this question: 'If feelings like anger and anxiety can produce sickness and pain, isn't it just possible that positive feelings like happiness, humour and laughter can help people live longer and healthier lives?'

From this initial question, scientists started to look at the impact of laughter and humour in a number of different fields, but the area of research that intrigued me most was the one that looked at humour in the context of attraction, communication and relationships. The results are as exciting as they are consistent: laughter and humour play a critical and positive role in each of these areas.

In Chapters 6 and 7, where we explored the rewards that attract and keep people in relationships, we found that a shared sense of humour was one of the factors that people regard as important, and this conclusion is supported by the things people say in my workshops. Shared laughter is the bridge that enables us to be more tolerant and compassionate towards one another, and it helps us take life in general, and ourselves in particular, less seriously – which are all qualities that both men and women value in a partner. Humour keeps a relationship alive and vibrant and helps a couple cope much better with the stresses and strains of everyday life.

Victor Borge put it very well when he said: 'Laughter is the shortest distance between two people.' And I will go further still. If there's no shared humour between you and your partner any more, you can be fairly certain that something, somewhere is seriously wrong. On the other hand, if you can both share fun and laughter, you have more than a 50-50 chance of keeping your relationship healthy, creative, strong and rewarding, because it's much easier for two people to share affection and love if they can also share laughter.

If you are wondering what a sense of humour is, it's whatever makes you chuckle and tickles your 'funny bone', that 'thing' that, as mentioned above, enables you to take yourself and life in general less seriously. What it is not is telling jokes.

Most emotions are highly infectious, both the negative and the positive ones. If you doubt this, think back to the last time you were with a whinger. After five minutes, any good feelings you had at the beginning were sucked out of your soul, your energy level dropped dramatically and you couldn't wait to get away. Does this ring any bells? And how do you feel after spending time with someone who's cheerful? Don't you feel cheered as well?

Can you now begin to see the connection between humour and attraction? In Chapter 10 we also looked at the various factors that influence attraction, and one of the things I emphasised was the importance of first impressions. I mentioned that we make all sorts of assumptions when we first meet someone new and that most of that first impression comes from what we see. If the other person smiles, looks friendly and appears to be having a good time, then we're more likely to see them as more appealing than if they slouch and look generally bored.

The research into what attracts people showed that laughter, fun and play are powerful aphrodisiacs. In fact, researchers identified three of the most important and sensual qualities that a potential couple look for in each other: a pleasant smile, good humour and a happy laugh. They also found that, generally speaking, men tend to respond to a smile, women tend to enjoy someone with a good sense of humour – and both men and women like to share a laugh.

Humour helps us approach people and break the ice. The reason I left it out of Chapter 15 on openings is that you need to generate your own style and not copy someone else's. One way to develop it is to pay close attention to how other people use it, for example, in films or television, especially of the 'boy-meets-girl' variety. Also, focus on what tickles your funny bone. The whole idea is for you to become aware of the things that make you laugh – but don't copy things literally, just use them as inspiration.

Socialising and dating can be extremely stressful, bringing out all kinds of anxieties. Humour offers a safety valve, relaxing the nerves and calming the butterflies in your tummy. And one last point. Humour is something that both can share and enjoy, and it's never at the expense of someone else.

At various points throughout this book I have suggested ways for you to develop a positive attitude and generate a warm, friendly and happy environment that will attract people to you like moths to light, but I bet I know what you're thinking. 'Yes, but how?' I've come to believe, as you can see from the previous chapter, that being happy is a skill – as well as an art – and as with any skill, it can be learned. You will find some overlap between this chapter and the last one, but there *is* a difference. To be happy you don't have to laugh, although when you laugh you're highly likely to feel happy.

The first step is to decide that there is another way to look at life, that you're not a helpless victim of fate. Start by asking yourself some simple questions:

1. *What does happiness mean to me? What makes my heart sing?*
This exercise is different from the one in the previous chapter and it's particularly valuable because it makes us aware of being happy. If I were to ask you to think of a time when you felt happy, I'm sure you could remember several occasions. However, chances are that you only recognise them when you look back but didn't realise it at the time. The more you focus on happiness, the easier it is both to find it and to recognise it when it happens.

   To make it easier for yourself, break the question down into each area of your life, work, family, love, education, leisure, hobbies, your spiritual life, and so on. Do this exercise regularly, say once a month, and consider every heading afresh every time. The past is gone and the future never comes because, once it is here, it is the present. So, all you have is right now. Make the best of it!

2. *How can I create a happy environment?*
Spend about twenty minutes asking that creative brain of yours to come up with at least ten 'environmental improvement' ideas. Again, break it down into 'bite-sized' questions such as: 'What can I do to . . .'
   - make people feel more welcome?
   - make people feel more relaxed?
   - make people feel happier?
   - make people feel more valued?
   - make my home more fun for me and my family?

None of your ideas needs to be terribly elaborate. Keep it simple. For example, taking the last question, 'What can I do to make my home more fun for me and my family?' Ideas can include switching off the TV one or two evenings a week, organising joke of the month contests, setting aside an evening to brainstorm ideas for fun and entertainment, and so on. Be as creative and as silly as you can. By the way, don't give me any rubbish such as 'life is too serious for all this nonsense'. Humour is serious business! Not only will it enhance your health but also your relationships. Would you consider this serious?

3. *What can I do right now to make my partner happy?*
   This exercise is best done together. Do this in two stages:

   1. Ask one another: 'Do we make enough time for each other?', 'Do we play enough?', 'Do we have enough fun and laughter?', 'Do we talk enough?', and so on.
   2. Discuss ideas that will help you have more fun time together.

4. *How do you respond to people's greetings?*
   If, when people greet you with 'How are you?', you reply 'Oh, so so!' or 'Not too bad', try replying 'Great!' said with a wide smile. If you don't feel like saying 'Great!', then *act as if*. Not all adjustments need to be major. Sometimes all you need is to tweak an old habit a bit here and a bit there so you can begin to change not only the way you see things, but also the way others see you.

There are many more way you can pep up your own life and that of your relationships. Here are some further suggestions from which you can pick and choose, courtesy of *Laughter, The Best Medicine* by Robert Holden:

Rise and shine!
The first few minutes when you wake up are the most important of all, because they set the tone for the rest of the day. If you're one of those people who get up at 7.45 and run out of the house by 8.00, gulping down your tea or coffee, still munching your toast, then this is definitely for you. Set the alarm for at least half

an hour earlier to give yourself plenty of time. Start by being as kind and gentle to yourself as possible. Create a routine that will make you feel calm and relaxed, and put you in a good mood, because that will make you feel you can slay dragons!

Start with pleasant thoughts. Close your eyes and either recall some really enjoyable event, or fantasise about whatever makes you feel good. You can also close your eyes for five minutes, breathe deeply through your nose, pushing your tummy out, then exhale slowly through your mouth and allow yourself to feel peaceful. Do this about eight times. Then switch on some music, move to its rhythm and hum along if you like.

If at all possible, do avoid the news and newspapers first thing in the morning. That's not the tone you want to set for yourself.

Fun time

This suggestion comes in two stages:

1. Set aside some time today to list the things that make you feel great, that make you feel that you're having fun and a really good time.
2. Treat yourself to some fun *today*!

Start a laughter record

Start a file recording ' happy highlights'. The purpose of doing this every day is two-fold. First, it will reinforce the experience and secondly, you can relive it at a later date.

Things to record include jokes that made you chuckle, the unintended or unexpected slip of the tongue, double meanings, spoonerisms that tickled your funny bone, a humorous anecdote, a thrill, a sense of achievement, a romantic adventure or silly story – they're all great material.

Donate a smile to a worthy cause

At various points throughout the book I mentioned that we're attracted to friendly people and nothing communicates this friendliness more clearly than a smile. The more you invest in smiles, the greater the return on your investment. Again, this suggestion comes in two stages:

1. Identify who your 'worthy causes' are. You might like to start with your family and friends, then move on to acquaintances, the milkman, the postman, the sales person, the garage attendant, your pet, your plants and maybe even traffic wardens. (Yes, they do come after pets and plants . . . but don't keep them off your list. They're in dire need of your donation.)

   Your donation need not be only a smile. You may have more things to donate such as a thank you, a cheerful greeting, flowers or a funny card for no reason at all, a compliment, kind words, or a special acknowledgement or recognition. If you run out of ideas, re-read this book.
2. Do it!

The kindness virus
This is a game. To play it go out and 'infect' as many people as possible with this virus. People remember little acts of kindness and love, long after you've forgotten them! These are the acts that inspire and enhance healthy, happy and loving relation-ships. You can set your own rules, for example you might decide to do one act of kindness a day, or you can declare one day each month, or better still – one day each week – 'Kindness Day' and score as many points as possible. Then challenge yourself to break your own record next time. Do it for no reason at all – and don't expect anything back. I believe this is probably the only virus in the world to which you never develop an immunity!

Three wishes
Play the 'Genie Game'. With this game, all players can ask for three wishes from the other 'genies', so everybody has to give

and will receive three wishes from each participating 'genie'. You can play with your partner and/or each member of your family in turn, or anyone you want to include in the game. I recommend that no more than three 'genies' play at any one time, otherwise it gets too complicated.

The three wishes are granted over an agreed period of time, for example, one day, one week or one month. Start with short periods and extend them gradually.

The challenge is to be the best 'genie' you can possibly be, but this is not a competition. At the end of the agreed period the players get together and check that the wishes were granted satisfactorily. Even 'genies' need to know how they're doing!

I hope this session gave you some happy ideas to make your own life and the lives of those around you more fun. If there's one consistent theme in this book, it's that it's up to us to take control and make a start. Take the initiative and make things happen so, if you want happiness, spread happiness; if you want laughter, spread laughter; and if you want love, spread love. The more of it you give, the more of it will come back to you. I guarantee it!

TIPS
- Decide that there's another way to look at life, one that's positive and optimistic.
- Invest some time thinking about the things that make your heart sing. Break it down into each area of your life: work, family, love, education, leisure, hobbies and the spiritual part of your life.
- Invest about twenty minutes to think of at least ten 'environmental improvement' ideas. Reflect about the things you can do to make people feel more welcome, more relaxed, happier and more valued.
- Think of ideas to make your home more fun for yourself and your family.

- Together with your partner, think of the things you can do to bring more fun time into your relationship – then put these ideas into practice.
- From now on, if you're not already doing it, respond to people's 'How are you?' with a cheerful 'Great!', said with a broad smile. Remember: *act as if!*
- Start your day by being as kind and gentle to yourself as possible. Create a routine that will make you feel calm and relaxed.
- Set your alarm for at least half an hour earlier to give yourself plenty of time.
- Put on some music; move to its rhythm; hum along.
- Find as many reasons to smile about as possible.
- Make a list of the things that make you feel really wonderful, then pick one and do it today.
- Start a file recording happy highlights, things or events that made you chuckle, gave you a thrill or sense of achievement; anything that made you feel great!
- Donate a smile, a thank you, a cheerful greeting, flowers or a funny card for no reason at all, a compliment, kind words or some form of recognition to a worthy cause.
- Play the 'Kindness Virus' game by doing little acts of kindness and love for as many people as possible.
- Play the 'Genie Game' whereby all players can ask for three wishes over an agreed period of time. At the end of that period, all 'genies' have to get together and check that the wishes were satisfactorily carried out.

CHAPTER 27

In Conclusion

Everything you read in this book had to do with getting new ideas and insights, developing new habits and ways of doing things. When we first start learning something new, or different ways of doing things we have to concentrate very hard; as we progress, the whole thing gradually becomes second nature.

Let me give you an example. Do you remember when you learned how to drive a car? Do you remember how hard you had to concentrate, adjusting the mirror, looking through the rear and side mirrors, changing gears, pushing pedals, steering the car, all at once? You probably couldn't even chat to the person next to you because it would have distracted you from what you were doing. And yet, within a couple of months, there you were, coolly driving in heavy traffic, listening to the radio or chatting with your passenger, and responding to a hundred and one constantly changing variables, all without a conscious thought.

It's exactly the same every time you learn something new. At first, you have to work really hard at it, trying to concentrate and remember what to do, how to do it, observing people's reactions, and so on. But, as with driving a car, it soon becomes a habit provided, of course, that you persist. So whenever you learn anything new, you need three things:

1. You need to know *what* to do
2. You need to know *how* to do it

273

3. You need, most of all, to really *want* to do it. That's the one thing that will keep you going, and persisting again and again until you get it right despite the occasional setbacks, until it becomes second nature.

Every new skill or habit needs time, persistence and patience to grow. Look back to the many things you've learned over the years, whether it was how to drive a car, how to cook tandoori chicken, how to play tennis, how to paint watercolours or how to fly, including of course your job skills. Do you remember what it was like when you were just beginning? All the times you got stuck and you thought you would never crack it? What made you persevere with some and not with others? It probably had something to do with how badly you wanted to learn that particular skill. If that's the case, then I have just one question for you:

HOW BADLY DO YOU WANT MORE AND
BETTER RELATIONSHIPS OF ALL KINDS?

Only you can answer this question. But remember:

IF YOU CONTINUE DOING WHAT YOU ALWAYS DID,
YOU WILL CONTINUE TO GET WHAT YOU ALWAYS GOT.

If that's what you want, then that's fine with me, but if you want more out of life, then I know that if you put into practice even some of the many tips and ideas in this book, you will make your world a happier, warmer and more loving place. Only you can make it happen – if you want to.

Sexual Awareness

Enhancing Sexual Pleasure

Barry and Emily McCarthy

ILLUSTRATED   NEW UNEXPURGATED EDITION

This book is written to show individuals and couples how to enhance their sexual pleasure. It is focused on feelings and fulfilment, and emphasizes a joyful expression of sexuality and intimacy.

The path to a new awareness includes chapters on:
The Pleasure of Touching
Self-Exploration
Increasing Arousal For Women
Becoming Orgasmic
Learning Control
Overcoming Inhibition

With the current emphasis on the importance of just one sexual partner, this is a timely publication designed to show you just how to make the most of that relationship, and how to build a new sexual partnership.

NON-FICTION/REFERENCE   0 7472 3561 9

SEXTROLOGY

THE LOVERS' GUIDE TO THE STARS

WENDY-ANN PAIGE

Sextrology is the brilliant new guide to the best way to find the perfect sexual partner through astrology. The sizzling star of the *Lovers' Guide* videos, Wendy-Ann Paige has used all her knowledge of love and passion to show what the stars foretell for your sex life.

★ **What are the sexual tastes of each star sign, male and female?**
★ **Which sign is sexually compatible with which?**
★ **What sexual delights does the year ahead hold in store?**

The answers to all your questions about your partner's desires and your future romances can be found in *Sextrology*.

NON-FICTION/ASTROLOGY   0 7472 4388 3

More Non-Fiction from Headline:

TEST YOUR BUSINESS SKILLS

J. MAYA PILKINGTON

THE ESSENTIAL GUIDE
TO ASSESSING YOUR BUSINESS SKILLS

**Do you have what it takes
to be a success in business?**

TEST YOUR BUSINESS SKILLS

consists of a series of carefully chosen tests –
so that you can assess your suitability for a
particular career, and your skills in carrying
out your job.

★ **Does your job suit your talents?**

★ **What's your management style?**

★ **Do you have executive skills?**

★ **What's causing a hold-up to your ambitions?**

★ **Do you have drive and persistence?**

The tests in this book will give you all the
answers to these and many other vital questions
– and not only help you to appreciate your own
abilities, but show you how to achieve greater
success in business.

NON-FICTION/BUSINESS   0 7472 3915 0

A selection of non-fiction from Headline

THE DRACULA SYNDROME	Richard Monaco & William Burt	£5.99 ☐
DEADLY JEALOUSY	Martin Fido	£5.99 ☐
WHITE COLLAR KILLERS	Frank Jones	£4.99 ☐
THE MURDER YEARBOOK 1994	Brian Lane	£5.99 ☐
THE PLAYFAIR CRICKET ANNUAL	Bill Frindall	£3.99 ☐
ROD STEWART	Stafford Hildred & Tim Ewbank	£5.99 ☐
THE JACK THE RIPPER A–Z	Paul Begg, Martin Fido & Keith Skinner	£7.99 ☐
THE *DAILY EXPRESS* HOW TO WIN ON THE HORSES	Danny Hall	£4.99 ☐
COUPLE SEXUAL AWARENESS	Barry & Emily McCarthy	£5.99 ☐
GRAPEVINE: THE COMPLETE WINEBUYERS HANDBOOK	Anthony Rose & Tim Atkins	£5.99 ☐
ROBERT LOUIS STEVENSON: DREAMS OF EXILE	Ian Bell	£7.99 ☐

All Headline books are available at your local bookshop or newsagent, or can be ordered direct from the publisher. Just tick the titles you want and fill in the form below. Prices and availability subject to change without notice.

Headline Book Publishing, Cash Sales Department, Bookpoint, 39 Milton Park, Abingdon, OXON, OX14 4TD, UK. If you have a credit card you may order by telephone – 0235 400400.

Please enclose a cheque or postal order made payable to Bookpoint Ltd to the value of the cover price and allow the following for postage and packing:
UK & BFPO: £1.00 for the first book, 50p for the second book and 30p for each additional book ordered up to a maximum charge of £3.00.
OVERSEAS & EIRE: £2.00 for the first book, £1.00 for the second book and 50p for each additional book.

Name ....

Address ....

....

....

If you would prefer to pay by credit card, please complete:
Please debit my Visa/Access/Diner's Card/American Express (delete as applicable) card no:

Signature .... Expiry Date ....